Down the Road in South America

www.downtheroad.org

Tim and Cindie Travis

Down the Road
in South America

*"A Bicycle Tour Through Poverty, Paradise
and the Places in Between"*

Down The Road Publishing
Indianapolis, Indiana

Down The Road In South America
A Bicycle Tour Through Poverty, Paradise and the Places in Between.
By Tim and Cindie Travis

Published by:
Down The Road Publications
2346 S. Lynhurst Dr. Suite C-101
Indianapolis, IN 46241
http://downtheroad.org/Publishing/

Photo Credit: All photographs taken by Tim or Cindie Travis except author photo on the back cover taken by Rick Gunn.

Dedication

I would like to dedicate this book to my older sister Debbie, I never imagined life without you.

Table of Contents

Map of South America
Our route

Chapter 1
What we Brought to South America

Tim and Cindie Travis

On March 30, 2002 we left our comfortable, predictable lives behind for a seven-year international bicycle tour that included thousands of miles, unforeseen dangers and dozens of exotic countries. The first year we traveled from Prescott, Arizona, USA to Panama City, Panama in Central America; that journey is described in our first book, *The Road That Has No End*. This book, *Down The Road in South America*, the second about our travels, describes the South American year of our journey, during which we flew from the USA to Quito, Ecuador and rode south from June 2003 to June 2004.

Although these books are sequential, it is not necessary to

read the first one to understand and enjoy this one. Information about both of our books can be found on our web site, www.DownTheRoad.org.

When we landed in Quito we were on track with our original seven-year plan with six remaining years of travel. But as the months passed in South America, the thought of being limited by time evolved into a new way of looking at our travels and we turned our trip into a permanent lifestyle. To date, we have far exceeded our original plan and, as you read this, we continue with our life on the road with no plans to stop. This book describes in detail how this transformation took place.

During the initial months of the trip we defined our journey by passport stamps, the number of miles completed and drawing a line on a map, but it did not take us long to learn the deeper rewards of travel by spending time with local people and learning how they lived. For example, being invited into a family's home because we looked wet, cold, and lost became a journey deep into religions, traditions and customs different than our own. Watching up close what people cooked and how they ate spoke volumes more about the places we visited than what can be seen in a blur from a tour bus window.

Traveling by bicycle placed us on the ground floor of society, but even that was not enough. In order to absorb the culture around us, it was just as important to have time off our bikes. Riding became a means of meeting people rather than a goal in itself. This new priority cut into our daily mileage, but we gladly made the trade; when we began our travels

Ecuadorian women in the Plaza.

in South America, we were not interested in the fastest route. Instead, we chose a meandering path deep into the Andes that guaranteed full immersion into the colorful cultures defining the region.

It was obvious that speaking Spanish would help with traveling in Latin America. We attended a three-week Spanish immersion school in Mexico, and then practiced daily as we rode through Central America. When we arrived in South

Cindie looking at a locally made necklace.

Cindie with Peruvian boys and their lamas.

America, we spoke Spanish on an intermediate level and could carry on conversations with the people we met. Conversations with locals are written here in English, but unless otherwise noted they were originally spoken in Spanish.

During our first year, we also learned travel could be dangerous. We had a few close calls - fortunately, without being harmed or losing valuables. Experiencing this criminal element taught us the basic tricks and habits of robbers, con men and petty thieves. We knew how to read warning signs by observing people's behaviors. We also knew city bus stations and tourist sites were far more dangerous than rural villages with no law enforcement. These lessons would be put to the test through some of the more unstable and risky parts of South America.

Before we left our home in Arizona, we knew we would have to travel cheaply to make our savings last by living on a total daily budget of US $20 to $25 a day. This was a huge adjustment for a couple with professional jobs, no children, and a lot of disposable income. We learned to copy the habits of locals by eating where they ate, shopping in open-air markets, and sleeping in the same hotels as truck drivers. Between cities we became experts at finding hidden places on the side of the road to camp free for the night. By the time we reached South America, we were comfortably living on a shoestring budget.

When we left home we hoped to publish trip photos and Cindie's daily journal on our web site, so our families and close friends could keep track of our whereabouts and calm

Cindie updating her journal in a hotel room.

their worries about our safety. Initially, we had no idea how to connect our laptop to the Internet. This technological convenience was not yet widespread at home, much less in undeveloped areas of Mexico and Central America. In time we learned it was more efficient to work offline, and then upload to the web site and send/receive emails whenever we found a fledgling Internet cafe. We expanded our Spanish vocabulary to include all the words associated with the frustrating task of connecting to complicated computer networks of the day.

Even though these connections were infrequent, extremely slow and unstable we felt empowered to do things we had not anticipated. We could buy and sell mutual funds, balance bank accounts, and even file taxes online while living nomadically. Our Internet presence through DownTheRoad.org grew beyond our wildest dreams and blossomed into our connecting with hundreds of thousands of interested people.

The first year of our trip abused our bikes and equipment, and we wanted to be prepared for the difficult riding conditions and scarce bike shops in South America. During our break in the U.S., I replaced most of the moving parts on both of our bikes including cables, chainrings, cassettes, chains, derailleur pulleys, bottom brackets, and headsets. I cleaned the bikes thoroughly and applied rust treatment and touchup paint to the frames and new tape to both handlebars. Along with four high-quality touring tires and several tubes, I bought a small folding tire to keep as a spare.

Knowing that much of our journey through South America would be in high altitude, we packed cold weather gear we didn't need during our ride through Mexico and Central America including hats, gloves, long sleeve jerseys and extra socks. To track our progress up and down the Andes, I bought an altimeter wristwatch that read altitude in meters. We anticipated distances between cities to be longer in South America, so we bought a higher capacity laptop battery and a larger fuel bottle for our stove. As if all of this bike touring gear was not enough, we also brought along both of our backpacks and hiking boots, as we planned to hike in Ecuador before we started cycling south. For an in-depth list of our gear, see Appendix A.

At the last minute, we threw in two books - one about writing and self-publishing a manuscript, and the other about how to get a manuscript accepted by a publishing house.

These few extra pounds in the bottom of my pannier planted a seed that would grow larger than expected.

The Road That Has No End finishes with us cashing in frequent flyer miles and returning home for a short visit. Six weeks later we boarded the plane for Ecuador with the lessons we had learned in the first year, knowing it would only partially prepare us for the extreme challenges of South America. The highest mountains, coldest nights, and the most dangerous situations were ahead.

Protest in Peru.

Chapter 2
Ecuador: In the Path of a Volcanic Eruption

Tim at the top of a pass in Ecuador.

During our six-week break at home, people asked me many questions about our previous year of travel in Mexico and Central America. I loved sharing our stories, but in the back of my mind were my own questions about the places I had yet to visit. The world is so much bigger than what I had experienced. I wanted to get back out there. I often asked myself, "When will my hunger for travel be satisfied?"

The answer should have been simple - a certain destination, a specific number of countries, a time frame. But for me, the answer was so elusive that I only knew we had to keep going.

We lifted off from Cincinnati anxious about crossing two

international borders. In our experience, crossing a border meant something bad usually happened in one way or another. The immigration process at an airport was easier than over land - airport border officials were less corrupt, even though we still had the headache of filling out forms and getting our passports stamped and cleared.

We were also nervous about flying with our bicycles. Most airlines require bicycles to be partially disassembled and stuffed into a cardboard box that seems much too small; we feared finding a mangled mess at our destination.

Years ago, I landed in Mexico City and found two bent chain rings (front sprockets); a few years later on our honeymoon, Cindie and I landed in Seattle to find ball bearings from our headset rolling out of the box containing our new tandem.

At the check-in counter in Cincinnati, we were unhappy to find our airline's new oversized baggage policy included our bikes. I called it the "squeeze the cyclist" policy, as its purpose was to make a pile of cash from people about to board a flight. It cost an additional US $260 to get our luggage and bikes on our flight to Panama. The clerk behind the counter remained cheerful as she robbed us blind. After paying for our bicycles I said to Cindie, "I bet in Latin America, a discreet US $20 to the right person would have made room on the jet for a couple of bikes."

During our first layover, we milled around Newark Airport and ate peanut butter sandwiches; we were too cheap to buy airport food. We overheard many different Spanish accents on the flight to Panama, reminding us of the world

Cindie's bike disassembled to fit in a bike box.

we were about to reenter. In Panama City, we were inspected at Customs because the cardboard boxes we used for luggage looked suspicious.

We had 18 hours before our flight to Ecuador. To save the cost of a taxi and hotel room, we laid out our sleeping bags in front of the airport's security office and slept on the floor. Nothing but the best for my wife, I always say! Cindie slept while I kept an eye on our belongings.

The Colombian airline advised us that we were over our weight limit, and they wanted us to pay US $5 for every kilogram (2.2 pounds) of luggage. When the attendant weighed our boxes and added up the cost on a calculator, it came to a scary number. I tried to bribe him with less money, but he refused. I complained, tried every angle I could think of, and then asked to see the manager. To my surprise, he was the manager! We negotiated and settled on US $280 to fly our luggage, including our bikes, from Panama City, Panama to Quito, Ecuador.

So much for my theory of always being able to bribe people in Latin America. After a brief layover in Bogotá, Colombia, we landed in Quito a bit after dark.

Ecuadorian customs and immigration went smoothly, and as we exited we walked passed well-dressed package tour operators holding signs with people's names on them. I was tired; I wished I saw my name on one of those signs, and someone would immediately grab our boxes and whisk us away in a private van to a cozy, safe place to relax.

Instead, we left the security of the airport behind and found ourselves standing on a dark street surrounded by beggars, con men and pickpockets, and needing a cab big enough to haul our two bikes and gear.

We spotted a van normally used to transport groups of people. The driver quoted US $15 to take us to a hotel listed in our guidebook. I knew from our map it was less than 10 kilometers (six miles); it should have cost less, even with the bigger vehicle.

He said, "Traffic is bad. It will take at least an hour to reach the hotel."

I said, "I can ride my bike farther in a hour" and offered him US $5.

He pointed towards the snarling traffic on the congested street and replied, "You can ride your bike and probably get robbed, but US $10 is the lowest I will go."

I looked down at all our belongings on the curb, and then at all the people watching us. My instincts told me this was not a safe place to be standing in the open with all our worldly possessions. I mumbled something under my breath (in Spanish) about the "Gringo Tax" and agreed to US $10.

Traffic was unbelievable. I often joke that traffic rules are merely suggestions in Latin America, and Quito was no different; it seemed no one drove between the lines or stopped at red lights. I thought we were going to die when we had a near miss head-on, and later when a bus almost hit us on the passenger side.

A recent heavy rainstorm had flooded or closed many streets. It took a full hour and a half to go those 10 kilometers. I apologized to the driver for not believing him and for my "Gringo Tax" comment. He told me to forget about it, and played Pink Floyd's entire "Dark Side of the Moon" while we waited in traffic. We had an interesting conversation about Pink Floyd, rock bands from England in general, and I struggled though translating Pink Floyd lyrics into Spanish for him.

I found myself liking this guy, even though I originally accused him of trying to cheat me. When we finally found the hotel and he helped us carry everything up to our room, I gave him the agreed US $10 plus a US $5 tip for being so interesting and helpful.

Shortly after he drove away, Cindie realized she had left our brand new guidebook in the front seat of his van. The hotel owner told us all cab drivers were crooked and we would never see our book again. But later that evening and

La Campania church in the San Francisco Plaza.

Discussing the news in the park.

much to our (and the hotel owner's) amazement, our cab driver knocked on our door, guidebook in hand.

It seemed we were starting out on this continent with a bit of luck on our side.

We woke up the next day to a completely new world. We had flown from nearly sea level to well over 2,800 meters (9,100 feet), and the effects of the high altitude were noticeable. Our plan to hang around Quito for a week before doing any strenuous activity turned out to be a good idea; the first couple of days, we were often short of breath from climbing the stairs and had frequent headaches.

We saw a few tourist attractions while we adjusted to the altitude, including the colonial architecture and historic churches in the old part of town. While walking in the crowded main plaza, we heard yelling and saw a young man running away with what appeared to be a camera bag; my guess was the thief cut the shoulder strap with a razor blade.

This was not a complete surprise - we had read about the high crime rate in Quito and shopkeepers warned us not to stray far from our hotel after dark. Months of traveling had taught us that a few simple precautions would encourage thieves to move on to easier targets. In big cities, I carried our camera under my jacket; Cindie wore a money belt under her clothes. Other tourists were not nearly as careful, and we often heard stories about crime from them.

One of the most popular tourist sights in Quito was a short trip out of town to the equator. The French had located the equator over a century ago, long before a geographic positioning system (GPS) had been developed.

Monument at the Equator.

Cindie buying souvenirs at the market in Riobamba.

We could not resist standing on the line that divided the earth in half and took a bus to the huge monument that marked the location. As we rode through Quito, we wondered if it was crazy to attempt riding our bikes out of this congested and polluted city. We paid the 50-cent fee to enter the monument area, took pictures and enjoyed the view of the surrounding mountains.

The next day, I pulled our bikes out of their boxes and reassembled them. After a complete inspection, I was amazed they had survived the abuse of baggage handlers in four countries. We put our bikes and cycling gear into storage at the South American Explorers Club (SAEC) in Quito so we could go on a few hikes. We had brought trekking gear as well as cycling gear on this journey.

Traveling without our bikes and related equipment was a change for us. We carried our backpacks, boots, tent, stove, and other camping equipment, and with our laptop computer in storage, we felt like we were traveling light.

A four-hour bus ride took us to Riobamba, Ecuador, where we arrived after dark and quickly found a room. The next day, we went to a colorful market with all manner of livestock, poultry, and handicrafts for sale.

We usually did not buy souvenirs because there was no room to carry them on our bikes. Cindie, knowing once our trek was over our backpacks and boots would be sent home, wanted to buy everything; I did not want to buy anything. We compromised on a few small wall hangings.

It seemed to me that Cindie had a need to decorate a house we did not plan to live in for a long time. I kept reminding

17

Cindie getting off the bus in Santa Fe de Galan.

Tim with the boys from the village.

her we were international drifters, without walls on which to hang decorations. I knew they would end up in a box like the pot holders she had to buy in Guatemala, but there was no fighting it.

We awoke the next morning ready to start our hike toward Tungurahua, an active volcano. We rode a local bus up a long dirt road to the seldom-visited village of Santa Fe de Galan at an elevation around 3,600 meters (11,800 feet). A crowd gathered around us as we retrieved our backpacks from under the bus. A couple of strangers in their village were a rare occurrence and they watched our every move, openly curious.

Several kids followed us as we walked through the village, giggling at my American-accented Spanish. They lived an isolated life high in the Andes; everything we wore and carried was foreign to them. I loved their innocence and curiosity. As our group of followers thinned down, two boys in their teens explained that the other kids had farm work to finish before dark.

Suddenly, I heard a loud noise that sounded like a fast-approaching truck. I jumped off the road and called out, "Car up!" in English to Cindie, a common phrase used among cyclists. She had heard the same noise and was already off the road.

The two boys stood on the road and laughed. The younger one asked, "What did you hear?"

"I heard a big truck coming."

He said it was OK; we could get back on the road. The older boy said, "I want to show you the big truck you heard."

Camping within view of Volcano Tungurahua.

We rounded a sharp corner, and dominating the landscape before us was a huge volcano, smoke billowing from its cone; there was a constant rumbling and pounding of explosions. This volcano could easily wipe everything around us off the map. We were close and could see the lava; it was beautiful and frightening. Our fate was in nature's hands.

The older boy said, "Here is your big truck. If it decides to come up the road, jumping to the side will not be enough." We all laughed hard.

As rain began to fall, we found a rare flat place to pitch our tent. I asked, "How long do you think it will rain?"

The boys had another laugh. The younger one said, "What you hear hitting the tent is ash from the volcano."

Cindie, a geologist, was excited at first to see an active volcano; but in time, the raining ash became annoying and messy to camp in. It quickly covered everything, made breathing difficult, and was potentially fatal to our camera. Our camp stove burned poorly because of the combination of the dirty Ecuadorian gasoline and lack of oxygen at this high altitude.

Once it was dark, we sat in our camp chairs and watched glowing lava exploding out and flowing down the side of the volcanic cone. This was not the first smoking volcano we had seen during our travels, but it was the largest and most active.

We heard voices in the darkness close behind us and turned to find an elderly woman and three young boys standing nearby. Because of the constant noise of the volcano, we had not heard them approach our camp. The woman spoke Spanish in a thick accent we had never heard before; she probably spoke a local indigenous dialect and Spanish was her second language. She was about 1.37 meters (4.5 feet) tall and had long braided grey hair.

She held a wooden bowl in her hands, steam escaping from under the lid; she said she saw our tent and thought we would like something hot to eat. The bowl she offered to us contained a mixture of boiled potatoes and what appeared to be giant lima beans. She waited anxiously while I tasted the soup; it was warm, hearty and delicious, and exactly the kind of meal I would expect people to sustain themselves with in this harsh climate.

As we were eating, the volcano made several loud grumbles and explosions. Pointing at the volcano she said, "Tungurahua must like you because she is speaking to you. The volcano has always spoken to me since she woke up four years ago. If she grows to love you, she will speak louder and kill us all."

Not knowing how to reply to this revelation, we simply introduced ourselves. When she shook my hand, I felt calluses on her tiny hands from years of hard farm work. Life seemed difficult at this altitude, in the shadow of an active volcano. The three boys were nervous and never said a word during our conversation. Cindie transferred the meal into one of our pots, and then gave her tea bags to take home. We said our farewells and they vanished into the night.

The cold and damp night air sent us into our tent and we buried ourselves in our sleeping bags. We fell asleep to the sounds of Tungurahua exploding roughly every 20 seconds. During the night it began to rain; we realized it wasn't ash as we discovered our tent still leaked. Several months before in the Guatemalan Highlands, we found a couple of holes in the floor of our tent we thought we patched before landing in Quito. Now, a good size puddle of water had pooled near my feet.

It was still raining when I crawled out of the tent at 10 a.m. to find a much different view from the day before; dense clouds engulfed us and I could no longer see the volcano, much less the other end of the tent. The rain had combined with volcanic ash to form a kind of sludge that blanketed the ground and our tent, like a concoction at the bottom of a wet ashtray.

We set off in drizzly conditions in search of a new campsite. As we walked through villages and farms, we saw glimpses of how people lived in the Ecuadorian Andes. Farmers lived in

22

Cindie with a local farming family.

simple unheated houses and toiled with hand tools in muddy potato fields. We quickly discovered our map was inaccurate and asked everyone we saw for directions to the next town. People were friendly and eager to stop, chat, and explain the impact of the volcano on their lives.

We realized the volcano we had come to marvel at, a beautiful force of nature in our eyes, was devastating to the local villagers. They said the volcano had not always been this active; the eruption and falling ash had started only a few years ago and now covered their crops and severely cut back on the productivity of the land. All the villagers had respiratory problems from breathing ash. Their farm animals had lost their appetites and were wasting away. Everyone who could afford to move away had done so; the rest were holding onto their family farms the best they could.

We often heard villagers say, "I do not know how much longer I can live here." I was impressed with their resilience and faith that better days lie ahead, even though their world seemed to be falling apart.

We walked all day, got hopelessly lost and Cindie became sick with exhaustion and a chill. As evening and another small village approached, I asked around for someone who owned a truck and negotiated a price for a ride to a place where we could camp with a view of the volcano. We filled our 10-liter water bag from a well and climbed into the bed of his Chevy pickup. He was true to his word and dropped us off at a flat area with a fine view of the smoking volcano, molten lava running down the side of its volcanic cone. Flowing rivers of fire seemed to be an arm's length away.

It rained hard in the middle of the night, but this time we knew where the floor leaked and made some temporary fixes. In the morning, it was still raining and now the roof was starting to leak. As it continued to rain late into the next night, we made the best of being stuck in our leaking tent. We studied our guidebook for South America and listened to several shortwave radio programs. After 24 hours camped in the rain in a leaky tent on a muddy potato field, we were ready to leave.

The next morning, we packed and walked in a light rain towards a village we could see in the distance. We wanted to be out of the elements and agreed to get on any bus to anywhere. While we became absorbed in yet another conversation about the dismal potato harvest, a bus came slogging through the mud; we boarded and rode back to Riobamba. When we arrived, people noticed our packs and clothing were covered in ash. They became concerned that the volcano's activity was increasing and were relieved to discover we had just come from an area close to the volcano.

From Riobamba we boarded another bus to Banos, a resort town well known by foreign tourists and Ecuadorians alike for its natural thermal hot springs. We spent nearly a week in Banos, washing off the ash from our equipment, enjoying the hot springs and going on a couple of excellent day hikes.

The rain continued to cause us trouble; during one of our hikes, we came across a raging river where the bridge had been washed away recently. We searched along the river for the safest place to cross and found a narrow section with rocks close enough together to step on. I went first with the camera bag and daypack, crossing easily with my long legs. Cindie, on the other hand, was scared to death. One wrong move and she would fall into the river and over a large cliff to a certain death.

As Cindie started her journey across, she stepped on a bamboo root and it broke. She panicked.

I yelled from across the river, "Keep going."

Wide-eyed and nervous, she jumped to the next rock and slipped before gaining her balance again. She was visibly shaken now and yelling, "Tim, Tim!"

As she neared my side of the river I lunged forward, grabbed her arm and pulled here safely ashore. She trembled and clung to me for a few moments; I could feel her heart pounding against my chest. It took Cindie a little while before

Tim above a raging river we would have to cross later.

The cable car across the gorge.

she felt calm enough to take a rickety cable car across the main gorge and then hitchhike back to Banos.

Once again in Banos, the constant rain made us lose interest in camping - especially since our tent leaked. We left the next day for Quito, promising each other this would be our last bus ride in South America while knowing that would be difficult to achieve.

We returned to Quito, checked into the same hostel and spent the next few days looking for waterproofing spray for the tent. The only thing we could find was seam sealer at a camping store, which Cindie used to patch the holes. We would not know if her repair job was successful until the next rainy night in the tent.

We retrieved our bikes and gear from storage at the SAEC and made preparations for several months of cycling in South America.

I spent some time on the computer building the new shell for the South American section of our web site, www.downtheroad.org/southamerica/. Cindie found a modern supermarket and purchased supplies like coffee, canned goods and peanut butter, knowing these things would be hard to find once we left the capitol. I double-checked the bikes, made sure all the bolts were tight and pumped the tires. We purchased detailed maps for the continent and face masks for the ride out of town; the diesel exhaust was overwhelming. We shipped our backpacks, boots and Cindie's purchases to my parents' house back in Indiana.

Quito is a large city of over three million people situated

Cindie pushing her bike through the Plaza in Quito.

in a long, narrow valley that stretches out for dozens of congested kilometers full of hustle and bustle, air pollution and crime. We decided to chance the dangerous traffic rather than ride another boring bus, because we were itching to get pedaling again. Cycling in a large Latin American city felt like fighting a war that was either lost or escaped, but never won. Losing this war meant becoming a hood ornament on a large truck. Escaping meant leaving city congestion behind and traveling through the famous Ecuadorian Andes.

We chose a Sunday morning to leave Quito, when most businesses are closed and traffic is reduced. We were trying to find our way to downtown and then south to the Pan American Highway, but navigating through town was frustrating; the lack of street signs meant frequent stops to check our map. Then, we had the best luck anyone in our situation could ever hope to have.

At a large intersection, we crossed paths with an organized bike ride of hundreds of cyclists. We stopped where a group of cyclists were watching a man frantically fix a flat tire, and asked what was going on. One of them replied it was the annual Quito Bike Festival; they were riding all around the city and invited us to follow. The route was closed to traffic with police stationed at every intersection and included several pit stops featuring food and musical performances.

It was not long before we were asked about our loaded touring bikes and our travels around the world. The local bike riders were proud we had chosen their country for cycling. We discussed their bike club and riding in Ecuador in general. They had the same concerns as riding enthusiasts back home, including better road conditions and rights for cyclists.

At the final stop, we asked for directions south. Several cyclists on sleek expensive road bikes offered to lead us through the back streets to the edge of town, and together we weaved through the city on secondary roads. Before we knew it, we were rotating through a pace line, just like on a training ride back in the States!

Our group rode together for 45 minutes, until we came to the edge of town. We thanked the group several times in Spanish and English - they had saved the day and we were relieved to be riding out of Quito without having gotten lost or hit by a car. This was the beauty of bicycle touring - a dreaded day of cycling in heavy traffic turned into a cultural event with newfound friends.

We rode on for about an hour, and then found a hotel for the night. During the excitement of the bicycle festival, we forgot to put on our face masks and found ourselves coughing up soot. We were alarmed to see how much black slime covered our exposed skin. It took several showers before we returned to our normal color.

The days that followed on the road to Riobamba were a beautiful introduction to cycling in the Andes; we passed incredible, jagged snow-capped peaks and traveled through deep valleys with raging rivers. Seeing snow this close to the equator was an unexpected surprise, and its whiteness added to the many different textures of the landscape. We stopped at onion and potato farms to ask for directions, and entire families would put down their hand tools to come and chat with us.

It was here that we got our first taste of what the big climbs were like in the Andes, with several passes over 3,500 meters (11,500 feet). Cycling at these altitudes was challenging; the thin air robbed us of our energy and our pace decreased substantially.

On a particularly long steep section, I tried to put the task in front of me in perspective. The optimist in me thought we

Cindie riding over a pass in the Ecuadorian Andes.

had been up longer hills in Guatemala and southern Mexico, where we faced three full days of climbing. The pessimist thought we were in much better shape during those previous climbs; the overall pain factor was higher now. Then the realist in me concluded it was a tie: This climb was shorter, but those inactive weeks in the U.S. had taken their toll on our conditioning.

During one memorable lunch break on the side of the road,

Cindie excitedly pointed at a truck overloaded with cinder blocks coming our way. Its driver was frantically pulling on the emergency brake and stomping on the brake pedal, but he could not slow down. He faced at least 15 more kilometers (9.3 miles) of steep mountainous descent. His only chance for survival was to stop the truck before it picked up more speed. The truck flew passed us and we jumped up to see what was going to happen.

The driver purposely drove his truck into the embankment and it rolled over on its side, throwing all the cinder blocks onto the road. We prepared to help and Cindie grabbed her first aid kit; but before we had time to react, several vehicles stopped to help and we knew the situation was under control. Three men crawled out of the passenger side window and stumbled away from the truck. As we finished lunch we agreed how lucky we were to be sitting where we were rather than at the first lunch spot we picked, now covered in cinder blocks.

Midway through another grueling climb a few days later, we saw it was about to rain and looked for a hotel. We asked a gas station attendant near a village called Mocha if there was a hotel nearby. He pointed up the hill towards the village. After climbing up a short and steep hill, we parked our bikes near Mocha's only church. Cindie went in search of this elusive hotel, but as I waited by our bikes and looked at this tiny town, it seemed likely that Mocha would not have one.

I asked an old man where we could camp; he pointed towards a grassy area and said, "Over there near the cockfight ring."

Cindie returned and confirmed my hotel suspicion. I said, "I have a Plan B - grab your bike. By the way, have you ever seen a cockfight ring?"

It consisted of a hole in the ground big enough for two roosters to battle to the death, and room for a couple dozen men standing around it. Luckily for us, it was not in use that day.

As we were setting up our tent a man walked up, introduced himself as Roberto and invited us to spend the night with his family. We walked to his house, where he showed us a room with two freshly made beds.

Cindie said to me in English, "This sure beats a front row seat at the cockfight ring."

We offered to buy dinner for our hosts; Cindie had seen a restaurant in town that sold roasted chicken. The chicken arrived at Roberto's home alive and clucking. Looking back, we should not have expected anything else; but at the time, it was a mild shock to say the least! The bird was noisy until we heard a loud CHOP, and then all was silent.

While Cindie helped prepare dinner in the kitchen, Roberto invited me to watch a video he recorded in 1995 about the war between Ecuador and Peru. This was not edited-for-television battle clips; it showed the real, uncensored, bloody story. I watched raw footage of a firefight with men being shot; medics throwing corpses on a pile of decomposing bodies; and a man who had stepped on a land mine getting his leg amputated in a makeshift operating room. During the film, I asked Roberto about the war between Ecuador and Peru; apparently, it was a border dispute between the two countries.

Tim with Roberto and his family.

The chicken foot Tim found in his soup.

Roberto asked, "Did you watch the war on TV in the U.S.?"

I said, "I watched the news regularly back in 1995, but I was not even aware Peru and Ecuador were at war."

He was appalled to hear this. "I heard that the war was not reported outside South America, but I didn't want to believe it."

"How long has this war lasted?"

He lowered his eyes to the floor, shook his head and answered, "Most of my life."

"Is the war over?"

"Yes, an agreement was signed between us and Peru defining the exact location of the border."

Sensing Roberto's sadness, I said, "In our travels, I have seen the aftermath of war too many times. The scars it leaves on the survivors are almost as bad as the senseless killing during the battles themselves."

Roberto said, "I agree; I have lost several close friends to this war and I still miss them."

The women called us from the kitchen that dinner was ready. I was glad to no longer watch Roberto's disturbing video.

We gathered at a large, round dinner table where a bowl of soup was waiting for me. I took a seat, looked in my soup and noticed a few unusual things floating around. I dipped my spoon and pulled out a boiled chicken foot. I glanced over at Cindie and noticed her soup was only broth, and that she was looking at me with a peculiar smirk. I fished around some more and found a heart.

As much as I did not want to eat these parts, I knew it was a great honor to receive them. As I gulped down the heart, I looked up at Cindie and said in English, "Tastes like chicken."

I told our hosts the story of a similar family in Central Mexico who invited us in for a Sunday lunch of menudo (soup made with cow stomach). To my surprise, they knew what menudo was. What I did not tell them was what linked that story to this dinner - namely, being forced to eat something considered odd in my culture.

The next day we packed, said goodbye to Roberto and his family and continued climbing towards a pass where it was close to freezing at the top. We prepared for a long, cold descent into Riobamba by donning long-fingered gloves, waterproof socks, insulated hats that covered our ears, and rain jackets to block the wind. I managed to hit 85 kph (53 mph) on the way down; it was a record that would be broken several times in the months to come.

Chapter 3
Ecuador, Continued: Escaping Thieves on the Road

Tim carries most of the weight over the passes.

Alausi, our next destination, was a two-day bike ride from Riobamba that cut through the heart of the Andes. A passenger train also ran from Riobamba to Alausi, and then down a stretch of track popular with tourists called Nariz Del Diablo (The Devil's Nose). This latter section used creative engineering to make the drop down the steep Andes to the coast.

While still in Riobamba, we weighed the pros and cons of riding the train verses our bikes to Alausi. The squiggly line on our map through the mountains promised to be hard work on the bike. The train ride did not require any physical work during the four-hour journey to Alausi, but required something more costly - US $11 each.

The spectacular section of the train ride, Nariz Del Diablo, was after Alausi. If we rode our bikes to Alausi, we could then ride the train through the scenic section of Nariz Del Diablo at a cheaper price and without the burden of loading and watching our bikes and gear on the train. If we had a time limit to our travels, we could have ridden the train and saved two days.

In Ecuador, we lived on US $20 a day including a hotel room; less than half that if we were camping. The road between Riobamba and Alausi had no hotels, so we would be camping for free and cooking our own food on our camp stove. Because the limitation of our travels had nothing to do with time and everything to do with money, our decision was easy. We rode our bikes to Alausi.

Little did we know, we were heading into a great and unexpected adventure - the kind of experience money cannot buy.

Leaving Riobamba, we climbed for hours until we turned off the main road between Guayaquil, Ecuador's second largest city, and Quito. The level of traffic, noise, and black exhaust on this new road decreased dramatically. We were finally on our way toward the hidden villages and seldom-visited places in the Andes.

In Ecuador, we did not see tractors or other farm machinery; the local farmers did not use horses or burros to pull plows, either. Farm work is done by manual labor from sunup to sundown. Most rural Ecuadorians are disturbingly poor. The prize at the end of the day for working so hard is the privilege of being able to eat potatoes and sleep under a roof;

Cindie ready for bad weather.

yet they manage to remain cheerful and we never heard them complain. We became convinced they must possess some long-forgotten secret to life.

I have known wealthy people who do not suffer nearly as much, but still find a way to complain about trivial things - the color of their bathroom or their pizza being cold. They do not know how to be content or appreciate what they have; they only dwell on what they think they don't have.

As I was digesting all these thoughts, it started to rain. The people working in the fields sometimes had a blanket to throw over their shoulders; most of them continued to work in the cold rain. So, instead of being miserable and complaining about the rain, I appreciated my GORE-TEX® raincoat. Months on the road had taught me to be more like the rural farmers of Ecuador - content with what I had.

The rain made the ground muddy and not conducive to camping, but we had to ride on and look for any place to set up for the night because it was getting late. I had read somewhere Ecuador was the most densely populated country in South America, and this rang true as people were living everywhere we looked. It was hard enough to take a bathroom break without being seen; stealth camping in this area looked impossible. We had learned it was safer to camp in a hidden spot than to be seen by others, especially from the road. We stopped an hour before dark and had no choice but to consider a few exposed spots that would have to be shared with several cows and pigs.

A young man in jeans and a gray jacket came out of his house and asked me, "What are you looking for?"

"I am looking for a place to camp."

"Bad men drive on this road at night, and there is no place to camp safely. A few months ago, two foreign men cycling on this road were robbed at gunpoint."

"That's awful, but it's almost dark, we are tired, and we have no other choice."

He smiled and said, "Oh, but you do my friend! Stay in my house for the night. I cannot have guests in my country being robbed."

This was how we met Enreano and his family. Enreano walked us to the front door of a house, asked us to wait, and returned with key in hand and his entire family - a grandmother, grandfather, wife, and three kids - who wanted to see the strangers from a distant land. While Enreano unlocked the door and led us into the house, he said, "This belonged to my brother's family, but they have moved away to Guayaquil because there is no work here. Where are you from?"

Cindie replied, "The United States."

He went on to tell us about his neighbor's brother, who went to New York looking for construction work. His family was still waiting for a letter from him; they did not know if he had made it or not and they were starting to get worried.

The house was empty except for one bare light bulb dangling from the ceiling on an electrical wire. It was a safe place to stay for the night and we had everything we needed with us, including air mattresses and sleeping bags. Enreano's family crowded into the empty room, watched us unpack and asked about everything we pulled out of our bags.

The second question after "What is that?" Was, "How much does it cost?"

We took out as little as possible while answering their questions and down played the cost. This family did not have much; only a few things were bought in a store, like the padlock on the door and the light bulb. We unpacked our beds, a change of clothes, and a Ziploc® bag full of peanuts and raisins. We were both hungry after the day's ride and shared our food with the family gathered around us. Their reactions told us they probably had never tasted a peanut or raisin in their lives.

The sleeping gear and new food were interesting to them, but the biggest excitement came from seeing the Ziploc® bag. Cindie gave them a demonstration of how to open and close the plastic bag. The women passed it around, tried opening and closing the bag for themselves and discussed the practical uses for such a bag. Witnessing this was enlightening; I had never thought of a Ziploc® bag as anything more than a novelty, but something we had taken for granted as common and disposable was a clever invention to this family.

After we were set up in the house they gave us a tour of the farm, including a large pen full of guinea pigs. Enreano explained they ate them only on special occasions because they were expensive.

He asked, "How often do people eat guinea pig in the United States?"

I said, "I have never eaten one. People in the United States keep guinea pigs as pets to play with, like the cats and dogs you have running around the farm."

He laughed and said, "You are being modest. People from as rich a country as the United States surely eat guinea pig every day. It's not practical to feed and take care of such an expensive animal just for a plaything. What useful purpose could a guinea pig serve as a pet?" He went onto explain that the cats and dogs serve a purpose; the dogs guard the farm and prevent predators from attacking our farm animals, while the cats keep the mice and rats away.

It was obvious Enreano and I had different definitions for the word, "pet." I reminded myself that a traveler never knows what could cause a culture clash or misunderstanding.

We continued to tour the farm and Enreano proudly showed me his prize bull. He described several aspects of the bull that I would not have understood even if he were speaking English, because I have not spent any time on a farm. As we were walking back through the house he said, "I have something special to show you."

We stopped at a locked door and he fumbled with an old key. He explained he was an Evangelical Christian, and he had recently received a full scholarship to attend the University of Havana in Cuba through his church; he was leaving in a few weeks. The church had bought him a new computer. I easily understood the leaving for university part, but thought I had misunderstood the new computer part. Since the few store-bought things in the house looked like they had been around for several generations, I thought a computer was unlikely.

Enreano opened the door and with a big grin on his face, showed me what was in fact a new computer. It was the only thing in the house plugged into a wall outlet; it sat on a desk made of cinder blocks and old wood.

As he pulled the dust covers off he explained, "I have had this computer for several months, but I don't know how to use it." I noticed after it booted up it had the latest Spanish version of Microsoft Windows and Office.

He asked me, "Can you show me what I can do with it?" I enthusiastically said, "Yes, I can."

We sat down together and did not move for six hours while we explored the operating system and software. I insisted he keep the mouse in his hand and made sure he was able to demonstrate everything I had taught him. My Spanish speaking ability was pushed to a new level.

Tim on the computer with Enreano.

While we were making calendars in Microsoft Publisher I explained, "You can put a picture of your family on your calendar if you want." He did not understand how this was possible. I asked Cindie in Spanish - we try to speak Spanish to each other in the company of locals - to please get our computer and camera. This caused a great stir among Enreano and his family; how could these luxury items be carried on a bicycle?

I took a picture of Enreano and his family and copied it to a rewriteable CD. Next, I pulled the picture into Microsoft Publisher and made his calendar.

Enreano explained he was going to Cuba without his family and he desperately wanted pictures of his children and wife to bring with him, so we proceeded with a family photo session. He printed one of them out and hung it on the wall.

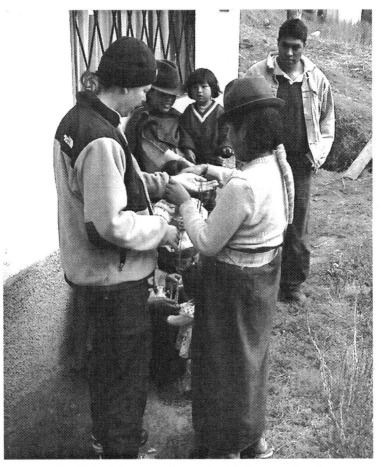

Cindie looking at trade beads with Enreano's wife.

When he held up the picture of him and his son he nearly cried. Obviously, it was going to be hard for him to be away.

We worked on spreadsheets and file systems together until midnight, when I went to bed; Enreano stayed up all night on the computer. The next morning he motioned me back into the room with the computer with several new questions that I answered, and then I took more pictures of him and his family.

I thanked him for giving us a place to stay and his family's hospitality. Enreano said, "I am only doing what should be expected from any man by helping others when I can."

He added that we were welcome to stay for a month if we liked. While it was a generous offer, we were already packed and the road was calling. We did not want to strain this family's limited resources. They would not accept money for their hospitality, so we left several Ziploc® bags behind as if we had forgotten them. We knew if we had offered them the bags they would not have accepted, but we were sure they would use them over and over.

Back on the road, it was mostly cloudy but at least the rain had stopped and traffic was light. Our road either climbed steeply for hours or descended steeply for minutes. I joked with Cindie that we only needed two gears for riding in Ecuador - the lowest gear for grinding up mountains and the highest gear for epic descents - and all the other gears were just for looks.

Because of these extremes, the locals had an interesting perspective of the terrain and their definition of topography was different from ours. We often asked about the road ahead of us and if they said it was "down," it meant the road may drop at some point but also contains hours of "up" as well. If they said it was "flat," we could expect to go up and down. "Up" meant it was time to be afraid - because "up" to these hardy people would put any Tour de France climb to shame.

At one point on the ride to Alausi, Cindie and I climbed to a small village nearly 3,600 meters (11,800 feet) high and stopped to rest and put on more clothes. I saw a man herding his sheep through the village and asked him about the road ahead. We were expecting to glide downhill the rest of the day because Alausi was below 2,400 meters (7,900 feet) and only a short distance away. He said he had walked the road countless times taking sheep to the big market, and it was "flat, then up - VERY STEEP." I wondered, "What exactly could steep mean to him?" We bundled up and coasted down a descent that we suspected would not last long.

A few kilometers from Alausi, the road turned sharply up. On this unbelievable hill, trucks either crawled at a snail's pace or pulled over to the side of the road because they had overheated despite the chilly air. Our lowest gear (22 x 34) was not low enough. Conversation between Cindie and me was replaced by deep, heavy breathing; I could hear my heart pounding in my head. My bike's computer showed my cadence (how many times my crank rotated every minute) was half of what it normally was, and my speed was 3 kph (under 2 mph).

At the worst possible moment, I heard my tire burst and suddenly go flat. We were in a dangerous situation; visibility was poor, with a sheer rock wall on one side of the road and a sudden drop down thousands of feet on the other, leaving little room for the large trucks to pass us.

Oh yes, one more thing - my wife was tired, hungry, cold and irritable. She accused me of being careless and not seeing the broken glass in the road.

I said to her, "Honestly, I never saw it. Why would I get a flat on purpose?"

I laid my bike on its side and removed the rear wheel while

Tim fixing a flat on the hill.

The train arriving in Alausi.

Cindie frantically waved away passing cars with a flashlight. Just then, the rain started falling harder. In the madness of the moment, the only thing I could think of to do was laugh.

With Cindie's help I changed the tube, pumped the tire and reassembled my bike. We were back to grinding up the impossible hill; once at the top we could see Alausi, over one thousand meters (3,300 feet) below. The descent was so steep we had to stop several times to cool our brakes.

The city of Alausi is located in a deep valley that drains eastward toward the ocean. The only ways to travel in that direction are on a pack trail with a burro and by train. We chose the train; as we found out later, the burro probably would have been more agreeable and less complicated.

The train that runs from Riobamba to the Ecuadorian coast used to be the major form of transportation, but buses and trucks have replaced the necessity of the train line. The train still exists only because foreign tourists pay a premium price for the scenic ride to and from Alausi, along the famous Nariz Del Diablo down the Andes. The passengers are allowed to sit on top of the train, and during our trip almost everyone did.

When we boarded at Alausi, the roof was already packed with foreigners sitting in the warm sun. We managed to find a spot to sit, hold on, and enjoy the view. The ride was smooth until shortly after we entered the Devil's Nose, when a set of wheels came off the track.

Because we were moving slowly, the train stopped before anyone was injured. It took over an hour to get the train back on the track and involved a local technique of lubricating the wheels with creosote leaves and building rock ramps to guide

Passengers waiting for the derailed train to be fixed.

Sunday market in Alausi.

the derailed wheels. It was interesting to watch, if somewhat dangerous.

Once we were moving again, we enjoyed the rest of the train ride down the canyon and back to Alausi. We stayed in town a few more days to visit the Sunday market and gather supplies for the road ahead.

Cindie broke the news to me that she did not like the food in the cheap restaurants in Ecuador when she said, "I am tired of rice. I miss Mexico. Where are the tortillas and beans?"

This was a shock to me, because I loved the food at the simple truck stops or small restaurants attached to houses. They ate well and could talk to a couple of tired cyclists for hours.

For between US $1 - $1.50 we would have a big bowl of hot soup that was brought out immediately, then a big plate of rice with chicken or beef and sometimes beans or vegetables. The soup often had things in it we were not used to, like part of a lung or chopped up liver, but we could set it aside.

The problem was, I didn't know what other choices were available. We could only afford what the working class locals ate. When the occasional restaurant had something more un-usual, like pizza, it was 10 times more expensive and these upscale restaurants added a 22 percent tax to the bill.

We compromised and occasionally we went out to a restau-rant that served Western food, but I was always disappointed with the small portions and high prices. Cindie often said I ruined her meal when I complained of still being hungry. We would continue to have this argument throughout South

America.

On the two-hour climb out of Alausi I had another flat.

In the cycling world, preventing a flat tire is like curing the common cold. First, it cannot be prevented; secondly, everyone has advice or a home remedy. Even though our web site was only 18 months old, hundreds of people were reading Cindie's journals every day. Anytime she wrote about a flat tire, we were flooded with emails containing recommendations for different brands of tires. I knew people were trying to help and appreciated their thoughtfulness, but sometimes flats cannot be avoided no matter what kind of tire is used. Ecuador had more than the average amount of broken glass on the roads. Avoiding a flat on the road was like a teacher avoiding a cold in a classroom of sick kids.

After repairing my flat, the road unexpectedly turned to dirt and traffic disappeared. At the top of a steep descent, I stopped to film Cindie riding down a set of scenic turns. By the time I finished and put the camera away Cindie was far ahead of me, which was normal when taking pictures. Because I was faster on descents, our agreement was that she would keep going and I would catch up.

I could see her in the distance bouncing along the dirt road, and then to my horror a rope appeared across the road, blocking her way.

We had seen this before in Chiapas, Mexico and knew the danger. Someone was trying to rob or extort money from Cindie by forcing her to stop. We had rehearsed a plan for this situation: I would take the lead; we would ride as fast as possible, and not stop for anything. If necessary, I would cut the rope with a knife I kept in my jersey pocket.

The knife was where it was supposed to be, but I was not. I panicked, shifted into my biggest gear and sprinted towards Cindie. Although I was picking up speed quickly on the downhill, I knew I was not going to make it before she reached the rope. She was on her own.

Other than the young man holding the rope, I could not see how many others were there. I kept thinking to myself, "They'd better not touch her." I saw everything happening but felt helpless to intervene. Cindie followed our plan and increased her speed as she approached the rope.

As she dropped her shoulders and prepared to barrel through, the man let go of the rope and lunged toward her; but just before he grabbed her, he saw me and realized it would be only seconds before I reached him. Instead of grabbing Cindie, he ran up a steep hill on the other side of the road. Cindie rode over the rope lying on the ground and continued to accelerate. When I reached the rope, I was surprised to see only one young man and a couple of boys yelling at me, "Siete, siete!" They wanted seven dollars to let us pass.

When we felt we were a safe distance away from the thieves, we pulled over. Cindie looked more frightened than I had ever seen her; she was white as a ghost and her hands were trembling as she squeezed her brake levers tightly.

"Tim, that guy tried to tackle me! I didn't know what to do. You weren't with me. I stuck to the plan. I didn't stop. I went as fast as I could."

I said, "I know, I saw the whole thing. I can't believe it. I was right behind you trying to catch up. Those bastards tried to rob us!"

"If you hadn't been coming down the road I would have been attacked. I could be dead right now. Dead on the side of the road or thrown over that cliff, no one would ever find me!"

"Cindie, calm down; we're safe here. You're OK now."

"What if there are more roadblocks ahead? This road winds up and down these desolate mountains forever." She sighed. "I want to go home."

Alarmed, I said, "Calm down. We need to stop and think; we need to collect ourselves before we make any decisions. You're going to be OK."

Cindie replied, "Do you think we should tell the police? I don't like it here. I want to go home."

"You know as well as I do that the police in a country like this are worse than the criminals. If we talk to them, they'll just want money."

Cindie finally started calming down. "Then what should we do?"

I answered, "I am going to find you a safe place to spend the night, where you can get your head together. It's going to be all right. Let's go."

After another hour of riding we passed a house where a woman was hand-washing clothes in the front yard. The water came from a hose that went over the road and up into the mountain to a spring. A few minutes later, we found a hidden place to camp where Cindie felt safe. After setting up the tent and zipping her in her sleeping bag with a book to read, I rode back to the house with our 10-liter water bag. I asked the woman standing in the yard if I could have some water and she called to her husband, who came out of the small adobe house and greeted me. He handed me the hose and said he saw us ride by. After answering the usual questions, I told him about our experiences in the Andes: Good people, bad weather, and the rope across the road. I said, "The best and worst can happen in the same day."

"You are beginning to understand the magic of the Andes," he replied, as if it was a well-known fact among locals. He went on to explain the common belief that whenever something bad happened to you, it would be followed by a good thing to compensate for it. If it were not for this magic, everyone living in these harsh mountains would die. His description of the belief's origins was hard for me to follow; it intertwined Catholicism with traditional indigenous faith.

He wanted me to demonstrate that I understood the concept of the "Magic of the Andes." I told him about getting rained on and not having a place to camp, and then meeting a family who let us stay in their house; he was not satisfied with my example and wanted another. I then told him that on a bicycle, climbing mountains was hard but going down was fun, and I added, "On a bicycle, for every up there is a down."

He had a hint of hope in his eyes and asked, "Is what is good for a man on a bicycle good for everyone traveling on the road?"

I thought for a moment and said, "No, it must be just the

opposite for a truck driver." They viewed the uphill section as good because the truck climbed slowly; they were in control and could relax. They feared the downhill section because their brakes could overheat and give out. I concluded, "What is good and bad is different for every person."

His face lit up and he said, "Exactly, in the Andes a bad event will always be followed by a good one, but what is good for one person may not be good for another."

I could have talked to this man for hours, but Cindie was alone and waiting for me back at our campsite. I bid farewell to my new friend. The last thing he said to me was, "The best and the worst of the Andes are yet to come for you."

Our conversation haunted me on the ride back to camp. Maybe there was magic in the Andes after all. There truly was no place like it.

The next day, Cindie was in a much better mood and didn't mention wanting to go home. To calm her fears about future roadblocks, we agreed not to separate on the road again. We continued to climb and descend mountains.

Although we had our guard up for robbers on the road we had other dangers to contend with and on a particularly steep ascent, a pack of dogs attacked us. Five barking little monsters came running down a driveway as we passed by. Cindie positioned herself so I was between her and the dogs, which were snapping at my legs.

I had been keeping an old radio antenna in my jersey pocket for such an occasion. I pulled it out, extended it, and started swinging; I never made contact but it stopped them dead in their tracks. The fear of getting whacked by my whip took the fun out of chasing me. This technique would work for several weeks, until we were challenged by what had to be the most menacing dogs in South America. After a long day in the saddle, we arrived in El Tambo exhausted and hungry.

After a sleepless night in a truly bad motel, we rode out of El Tambo and Cindie felt weak and complained of dizziness; she had trouble making the handful of kilometers to Canar, where there would be several hotels. The strong headwind contributed to ending the day early. We stayed in town to get a good meal and let Cindie's health improve in preparation for the next day's big climb to Cuenca.

After a good night's sleep, we stopped at a market on our way out of Canar and Cindie bought food for lunch. While I waited with our bikes a crowd gathered around me - a common occurrence in these remote towns.

The crowd was mostly old men and women, who were no longer bothered with shyness. When a person grows old in this culture they are not expected to work in the fields; instead, they sell the family's goods in the market and thus are experts at bargaining and making deals. The cute little old lady working her vegetable stand would talk you out of the shirt on your back if you let her.

An old man asked me, "How much does your bike weigh?"

I replied, "About 40 kilos (88 pounds)."

I don't think these small people had ever seen anyone as big as me. A gray-haired old woman reached up, squeezed my arm, and said, "You can come home with me and work in my fields."

The man next to her said, "I don't know, how much food do you think he eats?" She stepped backed, looked up into my eyes and calculated my grocery bill; something resembling fear crossed her face.

Cindie returned with several bags of food. I introduced her as my wife, and they all shook her hand. The old woman who was wondering about my food consumption remarked, "How does she feed him?"

She watched Cindie load my bike with our food; I watched her take inventory. Cindie noticed her watching and said, "This is our lunch."

"All that for just one lunch!"

Cindie chuckled, pointed at my bike and said, "Yes, he can eat a lot, but he can carry all this weight over the pass, too."

Several people in the crowd told us it was not a good day to ride to Cuenca; but because we were packed up and saw patches of blue sky, we decided to go anyway. Looking back, we should have listened to them. It was foolish to leave Canar and attempt the high pass in questionable weather.

As we rode up the mountain it began to rain lightly. After we passed the 3,300-meter point (10,800 feet), it began to pour. We stopped under the overhang of a building and tried to wait out the storm. We told each other it would be dry on the other side, which turned out to be a bad assumption.

We continued to climb up the mountain. The rain pounded so hard we could not hear each other without yelling, and

Tim leaving Canar in the rain.

there was absolutely no place to take shelter. The climate was too harsh to allow trees or much else to grow. We were elated when we reached the pass, but our joy soon faded: The weather was worse on the other side. In addition to the cold rain, a thick fog cut our visibility to nothing.

We descended slowly because we could not see the road ahead and did not know if it would turn to dirt, contain big potholes, or be washed out altogether. We were both wet to the bone and shivering. At the steepest part of the descent,

59

Cathedral in Cuenca.

The street our hotel was on in Cuenca.

my front brake cable loosened and left me with only my rear brake, which was too wet to restrain the weight of both my bike and me.

I could not stay behind Cindie any longer. I zoomed past her and yelled, "On your left!" I was certain the pounding rain drowned out my voice. As I continued to pick up speed I looked for a soft place to crash; I remembered the cinder block truck driver, who purposely wrecked on a steep descent a few weeks earlier.

After a few hair-raising turns the initial panic faded and I thought of solutions. To create more wind drag, I opened my raincoat; it helped some, but not enough. Next I reached down with my left hand and squeezed the front brakes together, while I kept my right hand on the handlebar to steer and hold a death grip on the rear brake lever.

When I finally was able to come to a stop, I was shaking and gasping for air. Cindie, who had no clue I had lost my brakes and nearly crashed, caught up and stopped behind me.

She yelled over the pounding rain, "Why are you stopping here? I can see buildings further down the mountain. We can get inside and warm up!"

I was still out of breath as I explained my ordeal, minus the part about nearly crashing. She held my bike upright while I tightened my brake cable. We descended for another half hour, pulled into a truck stop for hot soup, and then descended again. We were finally below most of the rain and began to dry out.

Only in the Andes have I gone downhill for a full two hours and disliked every minute of it.

We arrived in Cuenca at dusk, covered in mud, soaked, exhausted, and cold. I must have looked pretty scary; most people avoided talking to me, except the town drunk and a couple of shoeshine boys.

We stayed in Cuenca for nearly a week, and spent hours wandering the streets looking at beautiful buildings from the Spanish colonial era.

While labeling pictures for our web site, Cindie noticed our power cord had developed a short. The computer was bound to have a problem sooner or later; we used it almost daily, and it had been carried on my bike since the first moment we set out on this adventure 15 months earlier.

We found a busy electrical repair shop that looked promising. I showed the boy behind the counter my power cord and he took me to the back room to meet his father, who was soldering on a circuit board inside a cell phone. He had steady hands from years of working on delicate tiny electronics. He said he could fix it.

An hour later he asked me to turn on my computer so he could test the cord. The damaged part was neatly wrapped in electrical tape and worked like new. He charged me five dollars, and we were on our way.

We left Cuenca on a surprisingly flat road through pleasant green pasture land. Towards evening, it started to rain again. We saw a construction crew building a large house; I asked the owner if we could pitch our tent in his yard.

The neighborhood kids came to visit our campsite.

He apologized for his house not being complete and said, "You can pitch your tent on the covered front porch, if you like." This was excellent timing - the rain was coming down hard by the time we got under the roof, and the concrete floor kept us out of the mud.

That night the neighbors' kids came over to meet us and stayed for hours. They patiently watched us light our stove, cook dinner and clean our bikes. Eventually their mothers joined us for a while, then took the kids home; they had school in the morning.

The next day, we packed and ascended into the clouds. It had started to rain again; we stopped under the overhang of an empty building and waited until it lessened. We were both feeling a bit depressed about the weather, but could do nothing about it. The cold, damp air gave us the chills. We could

Tim eating soup in a local restaurant.

see our breath.

Cindie asked, "Will we ever see the sun again?"

The hard work on the bike warmed us up, but as we climbed higher into the mountains the temperature fell. When it started raining again, it came down hard and did not look like it would clear. We frantically looked for cover but in the higher elevations there were few buildings and no trees.

We turned a corner and through the mist, we could barely make out in the distance - a truck stop with a restaurant. This was the first place with food we had seen all day. We sat down, ordered two large bowls of hot chicken soup and reviewed our map.

There were no towns with hotels where we could reach by nightfall. As we ate, it started to rain harder. Cindie and I reached the same conclusion at the same time; we were tired from climbing all day and could not go on.

Although making camp in the downpour was a miserable prospect, it was better than riding in the rain. I asked the woman behind the counter if we could camp someplace under a roof. She had several buildings in her yard and plenty of porches; probably even an extra room. I added that we were willing to pay.

She said her husband was gone for several days and she could not make such a decision without his approval. Cindie was visibly irritated and mumbled a comment to me in English about the lack of equal rights of women in this society.

We sat and discussed our only option; we had to ride in the cold rain until we found a flat piece of ground to set up camp. Cindie was trying to be strong, but she was holding back her tears. It truly was a miserable situation.

We were finishing the last of our hot food when a young truck driver stopped in, bought a single cigarette and sat at the table next to ours. He saw our bikes and asked the usual questions - where we were from, where we were going. He commented it was getting late and we were a long way from a hotel.

He asked, "Where are you going to spend the night?"

I pointed into the rain and said, "We have a tent."

He replied, "I have room in my truck and I am going to a town with a hotel. Would you like a ride?"

Bicycle tourists tend to believe that taking motorized transportation is cheating. Occasionally I fall into this trap as well and for a moment, I considered turning down his offer.

We were both cold and wet; we risked hypothermia. We could have found a place to pitch the tent and survived, but the goal of our trip was not to draw a line on a map; it was to experience the culture. I did not want to let my foolish pride potentially end our trip. It was better to get in the truck.

Looking back, it is decisions like this that kept us on the road for years to come.

We rearranged boxes in the back of the truck to make space for our bikes. Before we piled in and took off, I bought a pack of cigarettes as a gift for our driver, Freddy.

It was well after dark when Freddy dropped us off on the outskirts of Loja. When the bikes and gear were removed from of the back of his truck I was horrified to discover my rear tire was flat. Too exhausted to fix it, we pushed the bikes into town. We learned it was at least 7 kilometers (4.3 miles) to downtown, but there was a hotel near the bus station just ten blocks away.

The hotel cost US $29 a night - expensive, considering our US $20 daily budget. I tried to collect the strength to fix the flat so we could ride into the center of town where the cheaper hotels were. Cindie sat shivering, depressed and defeated. We were still wet and cold; it was dark, and past our bedtime.

Was this enough of an emergency to splurge, or was I just being lazy and looking for a reason not to fix my flat?

Then I thought about Cindie. She had dealt with an awful lot in the past 12 hours, and except for a few tears, she never complained through all the wet and cold. Now, here she was willing to wait for me to fix my flat so another hour could be spent looking for a cheaper room. She was one of a kind; who else would follow me around the world on a bicycle?

My heart lifted as I remembered something important. "Tomorrow is our wedding anniversary. How would you like to stay here at the Ritz?"

"I would love it!" She smiled; she was the happiest girl alive. We pushed our bikes in the hotel lobby and asked for a room.

A couple walked past us in fine dress clothes, most likely on their way to a candlelit dinner; we looked like we had been through a war. Employees helped carry our muddy mess up the stairs to our room, which had little soaps, shampoos and Cindie's favorite - large, clean towels. We took long hot showers and went to bed. After sleeping ten hours straight, we awoke on our fifth wedding anniversary clean, safe and dry. I leisurely fixed my flat as we watched CNN in English. We would have loved to stay forever, but check out time was 12:00 p.m.; we left at 11:59.

The first major descent after Loja started in a cold, windy mountain pass and we put on our winter gear. We dropped 1,525 meters (5,000 feet) and because the road was in good condition, I could let go of my brakes and allow the bike to run free. I hit a speed well above the posted limit - but who was counting? We finally came to a stop in a hot, dry desert, still bundled from head to toe in warm clothing.

The next day we climbed for five hours and found ourselves back in the chilly mountains. This pattern continued for several more days to the Peruvian border, and was how the Ecuadorian Andes toyed with us before it said goodbye.

Central Plaza in Loja.

We would reenter the magical Andes again in central Peru, after crossing a vast desert for several weeks.

Fifty kilometers (31 miles) before the border, we approached an Ecuadorian military checkpoint. By this time we were low in altitude, riding through a hot red rock desert in the middle of nowhere. The head guard demanded we sit down and wait for his return. We thought we were being detained, which scared us; we did not know what we had done wrong, or what would happen next.

Our fear quickly disappeared when he returned with a big plate of goat cheese and bread. We hung out with the officers for hours, waiting out the heat of midday. I could tell they were bored and enjoyed someone new to talk to. When it cooled off enough to ride, we filled our 10-liter water bag, rode a few kilometers and found a place to camp. At the

Conochacha near the Ecuador/Peru border.

border town of Macara, Ecuador we made our final preparations to enter Peru and cross the large northern desert.

Setting up camp in the Ecuadorian Andes.

Local Ecuadorians driving by our lunch stop.

Chapter 4
Peru: Money Can't Buy Happiness, But Poverty Can't Buy Anything

Tim crossing the border from Ecuador into Peru.

Entering Peru marked our journey's eighth international border crossing since we left Arizona. It was common to hear warnings about each new country before we entered, but the warnings we heard from Ecuadorians about crime in Peru were constant and frightening.

Peru and Ecuador had a history of hostility and war; some of these warnings could have stemmed from that. It made us nervous, but we crossed the border anyway. If others had ridden through Peru, so could we. The desire to learn the truth outweighed the perceived risk.

Cindie usually handled our paperwork at the border; I was prone to absent-mindedness and known to lose important documents. While checking out of Ecuador, the immigration official asked Cindie, "Where are your tourist cards?"

When I heard her say, "What tourist cards?" I thought, "Oh boy! We're in trouble now."

As the official watched Cindie frantically shuffle through our papers, he asked, "Did you fly in?"

"Yes, we did."

"We don't always hand them out at the airport," he said, and to Cindie's relief gave us an exit stamp in our passports.

The Peruvian side of the border did not have any crowds. Cindie had our 90-day stamps validated so quickly, I never had a chance to get off my bike!

I commented to a moneychanger about the absence of pickpockets hanging around. He answered, "They only show up when the tour groups or big international buses are scheduled to cross."

Wow, what an honest answer. Avoiding the predictable large crowds that thieves needed to work was yet another advantage to traveling independently by bicycle.

As we rode into Peru, we noticed the differences immediately. We thought the extreme poverty was a side effect of being near the international border, but we soon realized how much lower the economic level was in northern Peru when we rode into our first sizable city, Los Lomas.

Our first task in a new country is to obtain local currency, and we were disappointed to learn the bank in Los Lomas did not have an ATM. When Cindie tried to get money at the counter with our credit card, they acted as if they had never seen one before. The teller said to Cindie, "How can you expect us to trade money for a little plastic card?"

Next, Cindie tried to cash a traveler's check; the bank would not take it, either. We both were shocked; who ever heard of a bank not accepting a traveler's check or a credit card? It's like a hotel without electricity (something else we would experience in Peru).

We had a real monetary problem on our hands. The closest Peruvian city with modern banking and an ATM was at least a week away. We had a limited supply of U.S. currency for emergencies that had to last for the next year. Cindie reluctantly pulled out US $50 and exchanged it for Peruvian soles, knowing it would have to carry us through the next week.

It turned out that our lack of local currency didn't matter; there was not much available to buy in the few dusty towns on our route. People who do not have money don't buy much and consequently, little was available in the stores. Common items in stores could be tied onto a burro, like sacks of rice, beans, and live chickens. On this stretch, villages rarely had electricity or refrigeration. We were glad we had stocked up on food before crossing the border.

This part of Peru also marked our temporary departure from climbing up and down the huge Andes Mountains to cycling across the flatter terrain of the vast desert that lay before us. Fortunately, living in Arizona had given us experience cycling in the desert. We had extra bottles strapped on the backs of our bikes for our increased water consumption. We started at sunrise, stopped in the shade through midday, and continued in the evening.

Tim with Rodrigo from Brazil.

This was everyone's schedule in this non air-conditioned environment. Fortunately, it was winter in the Southern Hemisphere and temperatures were uncomfortably hot for only four hours a day.

We had also entered a malaria zone without preventative medicine; we could not find anti-malaria drugs in Ecuadorian pharmacies. Cindie worried about mosquito bites whenever we entered heavily irrigated areas.

After leaving Los Lomas, we came across a bike tourist entertaining a large group of people on the side of the road. He had a long bamboo pole attached to the back of his bike with the flags of several Latin American nations hanging from it. He looked worn out; he had done some hard traveling and was sun baked from living outdoors. I could not understand him, even though it sounded like he was speaking Spanish.

A man in the crowd told me no one understood him - he was from Brazil and spoke Portuguese.

That sure didn't stop him from talking incessantly. From the ten words he knew in Spanish, I learned his name was Rodrigo and he had been drifting around South America for over five years. He pulled a large scrapbook from a bag on his bike and showed us clippings, including a picture in a São Paulo newspaper of a younger, heavier cyclist. Apparently, he was well known in the Brazilian press and neighboring countries.

I would have loved to camp with him, but we were traveling in opposite directions. As we parted, he pulled out a crumpled piece of paper with an address in Trujillo, Peru on it and insisted we take it. Fortunately, the note was written in Spanish. It read, "La Casa De Ciclista" (The Cyclist's House) and invited all passing bike tourists to stay. Through hand motions, Rodrigo conveyed that it was important for us to find this address in Trujillo.

In the town of Tambo Grande we saw shocking poverty, blowing trash and rows of rundown buildings. To make things worse, the main street was an unfinished construction project of dust and missing bridges. No one had running water; few had electricity.

People in the rural areas of poorer Latin American countries often collected water from rivers, but in the cities they usually had plumbing and taps. This was not the case in Tambo Grande; their water was delivered by a man leading a burro pulling a homemade cart with 55-gallon drums of river water. He would fill people's water containers for a few

Cindie riding in a rural area of northern Peru.

A small donkey hauling a very large load.

cents. When we collected water in Tambo Grande for camping, I was glad we had a water filter. A few years ago, I read Peru had had a cholera outbreak; now, I understood how this could happen.

Cindie was hungry and bought some fire-baked bread for US $0.15, but lost her appetite when she noticed the constant swarming of flies. When we asked for directions, a crowd of thin, sickly people quickly formed around us. The scene was medieval and hard to accept as reality. There was so much disease and suffering; we wondered how much longer they could survive.

The most difficult days on this bicycle trip had nothing to do with distance or weather; they were the ones in which the inequalities of humanity stared us in the face.

I believe it is true that money cannot buy happiness. After visiting Tambo Grande, I now know that poverty cannot buy anything.

As we crossed the desert over the next several days, we rode on poorly maintained dirt roads with washed out bridges and traveled through several remote villages where the streets were crowded with burros, goats, chickens and pigs. The locals, who stared from a distance but were hesitant to speak to us, had seen few if any foreigners.

One evening in the desert, just after starting the stove for dinner, about 25 noisy goats passed through our camp. Soon after, a family of goat herders cautiously approached us. Initially they were afraid, but became friendly after I exchanged greetings with their father. Curiosity replaced fear and soon the family of five became fascinated by our camp stove and

Cindie's digital watch. This family had few possessions; they did not even have many goats, because the land had been overgrazed.

Sylvania, the mother, told us there was no work in town, no money, and too many people living off the land. I felt like a king with all my pots and pans, clothes, fancy bikes and store bought food. Poverty was an uncomfortable thing to see; yet here I was, literally shaking hands with it again. We would have talked to the family longer, but they had to chase their goats out of the roadway and take them home.

We could see the stars perfectly that night. As I lay in my sleeping bag, staring up at the sky, I wondered who else was looking at those same stars. Were they OK? Did they have enough to eat? Were their children crying? I could only imagine the answers.

The next morning we were up well before the sun and lit candles for light. We made breakfast and packed as we listened to the BBC News on our shortwave radio.

While riding on this lonely stretch of road, two objects approached in the distance.

"Could that be a burro train?" Cindie asked.

"The semi truck of the desert? It's possible." It was too slow to be a motorcycle. As the objects came closer, I saw legs turning pedals and bike bags.

"Hey Cindie, they're a couple of bike tourists!" When they came closer, we all stopped to talk.

We had learned months ago in Mexico not to assume everyone who looked foreign spoke English. It was better to

Our campsite near the river.

greet one another in Spanish, and then sort out if it was appropriate to switch to English. It was common for us to speak to people from France, Italy, or Japan entirely in Spanish.

We spoke for some time in Spanish with Phillip and Violaine from France until they learned our nationality and broke into English. They had been on a bike tour around the world for the past 12 months and had been to Africa, Southeast Asia and New Zealand. They were riding to Quito on the same route we had ridden; we were following their route south. We exchanged information about road conditions, places to stay, the endless Andean climbs, and wind directions. We took pictures together, exchanged emails and web site addresses, sadly said adios and rode on.

That night we found a wonderful place to camp overlooking a river valley and off in the distance, the Andes. We sat in silence watching the sunset. Andean Condors ruled the sky above us, playing with the air that rose from the desert floor the same way their ancestors had, long before paved roads existed.

We were eager to reach Olmos, as it had a hotel - our first in Peru. Camping for three nights in the desert where water was scarce did not allow us the luxury of taking baths or doing laundry. We reverted to our standard arrival plan of riding to the central plaza together, where I watched the bikes while Cindie searched for an acceptable hotel.

Shortly after she left, a large crowd gathered around me. It was innocent enough at first, with a few interested towns-people; but soon the ranks swelled with unruly boys and drunken men. I could see them scanning our bikes, zeroing in on the various zippers on our bags and urging one another to "go for it."

Life on the road had taught me a few tricks; I was no longer a rookie. The game was on, even though I didn't want to play. I grabbed my handlebar bag that contained our camera and held it tightly, like a running back clutching an American football. This helped, but the real danger of losing equipment from the bike bags still existed.

I distracted them by telling them a crazy, made-up story about how a bear had chased us across Canada. They all listened as if we were around a campfire. While I was telling my story, making loud bear growls and grunts, I laid my bike down on its side and stacked Cindie's bike on top. This maneuver reduced the number of bags I had to watch from eight to two, but still my eyes were glued to our belongings.

The kids in the crowd tried to divert my attention by asking me to look over my shoulder at something they wanted me to see. The crowd was pressing in close and the situation was getting out of control. I wished for Cindie to return quickly, so we could jump on our bikes and speed away.

I heard a commotion in the crowd, saw two adults forcefully pushing their way through the mob to me and was relieved to see the newcomers were the local police. They barked out commands to back away from our bikes, first in Spanish and then in a local dialect I did not understand. The crowd complied and gave me space.

An officer walked up to me and asked, "Did anyone take anything from your bikes or your pockets?"

I looked at our exposed bags and replied, "No, I don't think so."

"Where are you from? What are you doing here?"

I said, "The USA," and explained that my wife and I were riding our bicycles around the world. They were interested in my story, although they didn't seem to believe it was possible.

Cindie returned to find me casually talking with the police officers and a handful of people. She reported she had not found a single hotel in town and was frustrated by people sending her in the wrong direction.

The police escorted us to a hotel and we checked in. Cindie commented it was unfair that she had to walk around town looking for a hotel while I relaxed in the plaza. After I recounted my ordeal with the rowdy boys, she no longer was

Tim pushing his bike through the market in Olmos.

interested in watching the bikes.

This would not be the last time the police rescued us in Peru.

We stayed in Olmos for two days, and the boys on the street behaved themselves once our bikes and valuables were stored in our room. Olmos was a rowdy town of hard drinking farmhands who came in from the countryside to party and let off steam. Normally we would have left such a rough place quickly, but we needed to rest and work on the computer.

The 105-kilometer (65 miles) ride from Olmos to Chiclayo went quickly, as the road was flat and we had a strong tailwind. As we neared Chiclayo, the traffic increased and we left the struggle of the desert farmers behind. We would now experience a different economic level in Peru.

We rode into Chiclayo and reentered modern society. The city had traffic lights and modern banking with ATMs; people no longer made their own clothes, but wore designer outfits purchased in trendy stores. Business people in suits carried briefcases and spoke confidently into cell phones. Family sedans and a swarm of honking taxis filled the streets.

Chiclayo had Internet cafes; I connected our computer for one sole (US $0.29) an hour. I updated our web site with Cindie's daily journal and the pictures we had taken since Loja, Ecuador. When I examined our site statistics and reviewed where visitors were coming from, I was surprised to see we were mentioned on several bicycle touring web pages and discussed on a popular online travel forum.

This explained the dozens of emails asking questions about how to buy a touring bicycle and our opinions on other related gear. People were noticing how long we had been on the road and were looking to us for information. The attention was exciting, but we realized providing advice was a big responsibility and something to be taken seriously.

During our brief stay in Chiclayo, we rode a city bus to the Bruning Museum in nearby Lambayeque. The museum has an interesting display of local art dating back over 1,000 years. An entire room is devoted to gold ornaments worn by the elite in an incredible display of workmanship and art.

We left Chiclayo and rode through the sparse desert again. Once we were away from the villages the flat, featureless, boring terrain made me sleepy; the only thing that kept my mind occupied was the occasional motorcycle that passed by. Cindie quietly drafted behind me.

For a split second, I actually nodded off while pedaling and rode through a pothole. The jolt threw our camera out of my handlebar bag and I woke up in time to catch it in mid air.

Cindie, who was riding inches behind my rear wheel, did not have time to react and rode through the same pothole. I found myself standing on the side of the road, holding our precious camera, not sure how I got there.

"What happened?"

"I fell asleep."

"Mr. Travis," my name when I am in trouble, "how can anyone fall asleep while riding a bicycle? That's just not humanly possible. Are you nuts?"

All I could think to say was, "Have you ever seen a sleeping dog dream they were running? Well, I was dreaming I was riding a bike."

"That is the craziest thing I ever heard. I don't know whether to be impressed that you are so comfortable on a bike you can fall asleep, or be afraid that I'm on the wheel of a mad man."

She went on and on, as only a wife can when her husband

messes up. I guess I deserved it; falling asleep at the wheel was dangerous, no matter what kind of "wheel" it was.

An hour later, we saw giant sand dunes crawling across the landscape. Cindie said it took strong winds to form sand dunes of that size and based on the orientation of the dunes, the wind was a head wind.

Twenty-five kilometers (16 miles) from Pacasmayo, the wind started to blow hard into my face and the trash from the side of the road flew toward us. A normal wind blew plastic bottles and paper around, but this wind was so strong it blew an old fan belt, a shoe and sheets of sand across the road. Cindie shielded herself from the sand blast by riding even closer to my rear wheel and warned me not to fall asleep again.

We slowly crawled into Pacasmayo, the wind and sand having burned our skin, my ears ringing as if I had been at an all-night rock concert. Cindie found a room for US $6.

The next day, we turned off the main road and headed for the beach. We rode through more rough dusty villages where kids yelled, "Gringo" at us at the top of their lungs.

A personal recommendation is worth more to me than an entire chapter in a guidebook. A visitor to our web site had emailed us and recommended Puerto Chicama as a non-touristy beach town. We always look for hidden paradises, and this place sounded promising.

When we arrived in Puerto Chicama, we went directly to the beach - our first in South America. We snapped a few pictures and enjoyed the sound of waves crashing on the sand. Puerto Chicama looked more like a fishing village than

Tim at the beach in Puerto Chicama.

Cindie with Chino and his family.

a beach town; its long sandy beach was occupied solely by fishermen repairing boats and nets.

A couple of locals in their early twenties approached and introduced themselves. One boy introduced himself as Miguel, and the other said his name was "El Mar" (The Ocean).

When El Mar asked me my name, I introduced myself as "La Bici (The Bike)." We all had a big laugh and they asked us if we surfed.

I answered, "No, I don't like sharks."

El Mar said, "Right now there are no waves to brag about but at unpredictable times, God himself has blessed this place with the longest left-hand break in the world."

His eyes grew big and his voice excited as he pointed at a piece of land jetting into the sea far in the distance. "From that point, if it is God's will, you can ride a wave four and a half kilometers to here."

"I'd like to take a video of someone doing that."

Miguel replied, "That is not possible. The waves are sleeping; the sea is for fishermen, now."

We said our goodbyes and pushed our bikes two blocks into town to find a room. There were no tourists; every hotel was empty. Cindie compared several places. They were all decent enough and around US $4 a night; she chose the one place that had hot water.

We rolled our bikes (sand, dust, and all) through the family's living room and kitchen to the back, where the rooms for rent were located. We felt awkward invading their personal space, but Chino Morano, the owner, announced, "Mi casa es su casa." (My house is your house).

We were not staying in a hotel at all; we were roommates with a Peruvian family.

We quickly got to know Chino well; he loved to talk and was an expert at finding out what made you tick and what troubles you carried around. Cindie loved his more comedic aspect, and I enjoyed his intense discussions about the meaning of life.

Chino once had a stressful job in Lima working for a multinational importing firm. Early in the 1970's he had enough of corporate life, quit his job, hopped on an old motorcycle and took off in search of the perfect wave and a better way of life. Chino was an avid surfer; he showed us dozens of pictures of his younger self on a motorcycle with a 10-foot (3 meters) longboard tied to the back. He had traveled for many years, working at various odd jobs along the way to fund his quest. His pictures of beaches and surfers were from El Salvador to southern Chile.

I spent mornings sitting on the family's deck overlooking the ocean, drinking coffee and writing a newsletter that would later become part of the first draft of this book. Chino somehow knew when I was ready for a break and would come up to visit. He wanted to hear more about our trip, and loved looking at maps and pictures on my computer. In the process, I translated lengthy sections of my newsletter into Spanish so he could analyze it. He was searching for something much deeper than entertainment. He wanted to know how the bike trip had changed my perspective on life.

Chino quickly zeroed in on my dilemma: I was determined to tell our story on the Internet, but unsure of the purpose of this effort.

He said, "It reminds me of going down the road on my motorcycle, not knowing my destination but flying full speed to get there. Your web site is a generous gift to humanity because it educates one part of the world about another. Tim, you are in a unique position. You're lucky enough to be born in a wealthy country, clever enough to understand the new (Internet) technology that enables the world to see your work, and creative enough to take all your experiences and represent them in photos and writing. The purpose of your effort will reveal itself in time; for now, just embrace the journey."

This was the beauty of Chino; he spoke on many levels. Mentors are hard to find for a traveling man, and I felt I had found one in him. In the end, he assured me a bike and a computer would take me farther than "just" around the world.

One afternoon, Chino showed us the remains of a pier that a huge storm had damaged six months earlier. It was used to export fish from the cannery, which employed 5,000 locals. Then we walked over to the beach, and he told us international surfers watched web sites that scientifically forecasted wave conditions. When conditions were right, they flocked to Puerto Chicama. The town had no Internet access, so the only way locals knew the waves were coming was when the foreign surfers arrived.

While on his motorcycle tour, he was the first to discover the world-class surfing conditions here and put this small village on the map in the surfing world. He said, "I traveled far seeking what was close to where I started."

The night before we planned to leave, Cindie woke up several times running to the bathroom. By morning, she was weak and sick. Chino was concerned; he had seen these symptoms before, and insisted we see the village doctor. We agreed and walked to a modern clinic where Cindie was examined and prescribed antibiotics we bought there. The entire bill for the medical exam and the medicine came to US $6.

We stayed another day at Chino's while Cindie rested and regained her health. This gave me more time to have long conversations with Chino. When it was time to say goodbye, Cindie was in tears to leave such good friends. We took a final group picture and straddled our bikes, ready to go.

Just before we left, Chino gave me a piece of paper with the address for "La Casa De Ciclista," the same one Rodrigo the Brazilian cyclist gave us a few weeks earlier. While in Chiclayo, we had also received three emails from other foreign bike tourists, urging us to visit La Casa De Ciclista.

On the road to Trujillo we met another cyclist, Hamilton from Brazil. He spoke Spanish with a few words of Portuguese thrown in, and told us he found work as he traveled around South America. I asked him how long he had been on the road, but he never gave me an answer; it was as if he had lost track of time. My guess is, he was a born wanderer and probably had been traveling most of his life.

I said to him, "You are a child of the road."

He grinned and said, "It is true."

In our travels, we have met a few "children of the road."

Tim and Hamilton.

These true drifters are a beautiful thing to see, because they had freedom, optimism and curiosity. I am not sure how they survive; maybe they work where they can or play music on the street. One thing is certain - they believe something will come along to help them to keep moving. For their sake, I hope it always will.

Hamilton was going to Ecuador, we were going to Argentina; we exchanged information about the road ahead. Meeting him made me wonder what years of living on the road would do to us.

We rode into Trujillo, Peru's second-largest city, looking for La Casa De Ciclista and stopped at a bike shop to ask for directions. Inside, everyone knew where it was. The owner sent his nephews to lead us there, reminding them to be careful of thieves near the market.

Lucho and Maurizio.

The two boys delivered us to a plain-looking house, except for a painting over the door of two cyclists holding up the earth; one was a road racer and the other was a bike tourist. One of the boys knocked on the door. Someone opened it and we were rushed inside with our loaded bikes.

We entered a world of bike culture and felt accepted among our own kind. A man wearing a greasy shop apron and holding a dirty chain tool introduced himself as Lucho, the leader of the house.

He asked, "Did you have a good ride today?"

This was our first insight into Lucho's priorities: Cycling first, everything else second.

Later, after a conversation about riding on the crowded roads of Trujillo, he asked, "What is your name and where are you from?"

When I told him, Lucho replied, "The USA is the home of one of the greatest cyclists, Lance Armstrong!"

A friendly debate broke out among the other cyclists staying at the house over who was the greatest cyclist ever. Everyone had a different way to measure such a thing.

La Casa De Ciclista is a unique gathering place for long-distance traveling cyclists from around the world. It is not in a guidebook, but instead passed along by word of mouth from cyclists who meet on the road.

Inside was a full set of bike tools and parts for a tired bicycle. Every inch of the house had decades of cycling memorabilia, including posters in several languages that covered the walls. Guests' touring bicycles were parked in every available space. Some were shiny and new, indicating the beginning of a tour; others were worn and abused, having seen their fair share of the road. In short, it was like a church for those living the bicycle lifestyle.

Lucho, his wife Arecilli and daughter Angela were our hosts. Lucho lived and breathed cycling, and loved the machine, the sport, the competition and the lifestyle. He had the kind of personality that created immediate and lasting friendships. Although he knew the names of bike parts in Dutch, French, Italian, English and German, he spoke only Spanish. He explained cyclists from different parts of the world do not need to speak a common language to communicate.

He said, "All cyclists understand freedom, the wind in their hair, the wheels turning under them, the sound a bike makes when it is tuned to perfection, the agony of a head wind, and the frustration of a flat tire. Anyone who

93

Tim riding through the ancient ruins of Chan Chan.

understands these things is welcome in my house."

We had originally planned to stay at La Casa De Ciclista for only three nights, but found it so interesting and enjoyable we stayed for a week. I spent afternoons helping Lucho work on bikes and having long conversations about anything related to cycling.

Over the years Lucho has had extraordinary people pass through his house, and he told great stories about them. There was the French couple who were traveling, had a baby, bought a trailer, and continued on for years. Or the 75-year-old Japanese man who had circled the world several times on his bike and had no intention of letting age slow him down.

We went on many rides, including a mountain bike outing around the ancient archeological ruins of Chan Chan that spanned over several square kilometers. They were difficult

Tim and Lucho.

to see on foot, but perfect on a bicycle. We meandered through the spectacular ruins and Lucho explained important places along the way.

It was at Lucho's that we met Fritz, an experienced bike tourist who spoke German, English and Spanish. He had quit his job in Germany as an electrical engineer to pursue the bike trip of his dreams. He had begun from a friend's house in Kansas and was riding south toward Patagonia. While reviewing information in Lucho's extensive library of cycling routes in South America, we realized we were going in the same direction.

Under the watchful eye of Lucho, our personal escort and guide, we left Trujillo with our new traveling companion, Fritz. We rode our way through dense traffic, passing two cab drivers in a physical confrontation over a fender bender as we left the city limits.

Lucho had to turn around, having ridden three hours from his home. This meant I had to say goodbye to a man I knew was like no other I would ever meet.

Standing on a windswept hill on the open road, I said, "Lucho my friend, when we are done traveling I would like to return for a longer visit. We could ride together every day."

Lucho grinned. "You have no appetite to stop traveling. When you two are done traveling, you will be old and gray."

"Then I will return to you an old man and we will ride together until we reach the final kilometer."

We hugged one another and repeated, "Until the final kilometer!"

The next day we took one last look at the ocean, turned off the coastal road, and rode inland on a dirt service road for a large hydroelectric system. Lucho recommended this route, as it was a scenic alternative to the busy main highway over the Andes.

We rode into a red rock desert so dry no vegetation grew. I spotted the perfect camping place near an aqueduct, with wide-open views of the barren mountains towering above.

Tim at our campsite in the desert.

This source of water was crucial; it would be a full day's ride to the next water source. That night we listened to the news on our shortwave radio and discussed world politics with Fritz. It was enlightening to here a European perspective of world events.

Then we began the biggest climb of our lives: From sea level to 4,680 meters (15,350 feet), crossing the second highest mountain chain in the world, the Andes! It would take two weeks to reach the summit, including a couple of layovers to adjust to the altitude.

It was a challenge to find a flat place near a water source to camp every night. Our water sources ranged from asking villagers to fill our containers to the rare spring dripping from the side of a cliff.

When we reached the outpost settlement of Huallanca at

Cindie and Fritz on the road to Huallanca.

Cindie riding through Yuramarca, Peru

Huallanca.

1,300 meters (4,265 feet), I stumbled into our guesthouse room and fell into bed. I had a high fever and felt sick. Cindie felt my clammy skin, switched into nursing mode, and pushed a thermometer in my mouth.

Mumbling over it, I said, "Where did you get this thermometer?

"Be quiet so I can get an accurate reading."

I pulled out the thermometer. "Who brings a thermometer on a bike tour? What else do you have in your bags I don't know about?"

She said, "Mr. Travis, put that back in your mouth, shut up and let me get an accurate reading."

I sat quietly with the thermometer in my mouth and she went on to say, "I have always carried a thermometer and a few odds and ends in my bags for medical emergencies. I

Cindie moving out of the way of a bus.

carry a lot of things you don't know about. Don't go in my bags snooping around and making a mess."

She looked at her watch, pulled the thermometer out of my mouth, saw my temperature was 101° F (38.3° C) and said, "Take these two aspirin and stay in bed."

Cindie stayed up late placing wet bandanas on my head and neck to cool me down, and didn't go to bed until after my fever had dropped to a safe level.

I felt better the following day, but now Cindie and Fritz both had a fever and were bedridden. We stayed in the village for three days until we all felt strong enough to ride again.

Leaving Huallanca, the road climbed steeply into another tight canyon with 36 unlit tunnels; the longer ones were so dark I could not see my hand in front of my face, and we navigated by feeling for the ruts trucks made in the dirt road under

Cindie and Fritz riding into a tunnel.

our wheels. In the middle of the longest tunnel, a rapidly approaching bus blinded us with its headlights. We dismounted and pressed up against the wall so the bus could squeeze by. In its wake we were bottled up in the windless tunnel with the dust and exhaust. When we emerged, we gasped for fresh air and our eyes hurt from the bright sunlight.

As we climbed higher, we broke free of the canyon and entered a rolling green valley lined with tall, snow-capped mountains. The paved roads and scenery were a welcome sight after days of grinding up dirt roads through barren terrain. We rode above 3,000 meters (9,840 feet) and into Huarez, where it was cold and hard to breathe. Yet, we were only two-thirds of the way up to our highest pass. We stayed in Huarez several days to acclimate to the change in altitude, and then Fritz, Cindie and I continued our climb deep into the Andes.

Two days later, we reached a fork in the road. Cindie and I wanted to explore a new road built by a Canadian mining company to supply a gold mine in the area; Fritz took a different route over the great divide. Our road did not exist on any of our maps, but we had heard it was paved and most likely at a gentle grade for the mining trucks. We made plans to meet Fritz on the other side.

We continued our ride up an endless hill and the moment my altimeter read 4,000 meters (13,120 feet), it started to snow. It was a bizarre experience for us, who until last week had spent a month crossing a desert.

At this high altitude, most people in Peru clung to life by herding sheep. Vegetation was scarce so it was hard work, with long distances to cover and longer days. Sheepherders always had several large dogs to help them protect the sheep from predators. The sight of Cindie and me slowly approaching their sheep set off the dogs' instincts to attack. Sheep dogs were different from other dogs that had attacked us in the past; their coats were thick and matted and they had a violent disposition.

During a slow climb, we suddenly found ourselves surrounded by six of these angry dogs. I pulled out my trusty radio antenna and hit the nose of the dog growling and

Money Can't Buy Happiness, But Poverty Can't Buy Anything

snapping at my calf; I hit him several times until it broke in half. He did not seem to care and kept coming at me.

Fortunately, I had a supply of rocks in my jersey pockets to fend off dogs I could not reach with my antenna. I threw one as hard as I could and it bounced off the thick coat around the dog's neck, but at least it slowed him down.

I turned to see how Cindie was doing and saw a dog snapping at her heels. I retrieved another rock from my pocket and nailed him in the leg; he yelped but kept up the attack. Cindie was now throwing rocks at the dog, too, repeatedly hitting him in the head until he backed off from her leg.

Four dogs remained, including the one snapping at my calf. The biggest one decided to lunge at my other leg, but missed and collided with my rear pannier instead. When he came at me again, I cracked him across the head with my biggest rock. This dazed him for a moment, but he kept charging.

Soon I was out of rocks; I had to resort to my last weapon. I turned my bike toward the alpha dog and sprinted to ramming speed. I hit him from the side, knocked him over and ran over his hind legs; he yelped loudly, but managed to get up and run. Since he was the leader of the pack, the other dogs stopped attacking us and followed him.

From this point on, we would suffer through daily dog attacks in the high sheepherding country. I argued with myself over which was better ammunition: 15 smaller rocks or five good-sized ones. The big ones would stop a dog, but I could carry only a few. The smaller ones lasted longer, but sometimes they only made the big dogs angrier. I thought

103

The sow's territory near our room in Conococha.

seriously about tying a machete to my bike, which would tip the balance of power in my favor during the dog wars.

We continued riding through the snow into Conococha, a miserably cold and damp village without electricity or running water. We found a room with two bunk beds in a guesthouse. The floor was dirt, and the blankets smelled of mildew; our tent would have been less drafty, and the wilderness offered a cleaner bathroom. Our evening's entertainment was chasing the family chickens out of our room that snuck in every time we opened the door. To get to the outhouse, we had to run the gauntlet passed a large sow that charged us the moment we set foot in her yard.

Once the sun went down we lit a few candles, but it was too cold to do anything but go to sleep and dream of snapping dogs and snowstorms.

Pachapaqui.

We climbed even higher over the next two days. The thin air made us dizzy, and we both had slight headaches from the altitude. The lack of air made the scenery sharper and colors more vivid, especially the glaciers and high snow-capped peaks that surrounded us. Originally we had planned to ride over the pass in a single day, but the wind and the altitude cut our ride short.

After our experience the previous night, we decided to camp rather than stay in another dirty guesthouse. We noted as we pitched the tent that this was the highest altitude we had ever camped, and it made for a cold and windy night. We did not crawl out of the tent the next morning until the sun had warmed us. We lingered a little longer than usual over coffee; it was such a pleasant valley to look at. As we packed, a couple of boys herded their sheep through our camp.

The next several hours of cycling were slow going and took a lot of patience. We made frequent stops to catch our breath. When we reached the pass at 4,680 meters (15,350 feet), we had a private celebration with ice-cold water and candy bars. This was our all-time record for altitude, including hiking; I never thought it would be achieved on a loaded touring bike and with rocks in our pockets.

We took a few pictures, but it was too cold to stop for long. We coasted down the other side and turned off onto the bumpy dirt road that took us to Huallanca, where we planned to meet Fritz.

The Pass at 4680 meters (15,350 feet) to Huallanca.

Chapter 5
Peru, Continued: A Bicycle Crash on a Dangerous Road

Cindie riding into a village.

In Huallanca we reunited with Fritz, who had taken a different route over the mountains. We knew the next section of Peru would be difficult - along dirt roads through remote villages high in the Andes - and Fritz joined us, as a bigger group was safer. We had heard some disturbing stories about the people and dogs in this area.

I wondered, "Could any place be that unfriendly?"

As the three of us set off from Huallanca, we met a German couple cycling with their dog in a trailer. They had just come from the remote section we were about to enter.

I asked them about the locals, expecting them to tell me everything was all right. Usually when we hear warnings,

Women doing laundry in the river.

they turn out to be nothing.

His answer was troubling: "All the people on that road are stupid. The villages are stupid and the dogs are vicious killers."

I easily believed him about the dogs, but it was uncommon to hear seasoned travelers call the locals stupid. I assumed he must have chosen this word without thinking, maybe because English was his second language. In time we would learn what he really meant.

The road out of Huallanca descended through a deep canyon and past several indigenous women doing laundry in the ice-cold water of the river. This was a common scene in rural Peru; having water run out of a faucet was a privilege only a few enjoyed. Most walked long distances to filthy rivers to wash their clothes and collect water.

Peru, Continued: A Bicycle Crash on a Dangerous Road

At the village of La Union, we ate another typical lunch of white rice and rubbery chicken. However, we did enjoy the coca tea. This tea would be illegal in the U.S. because it was made from the leaves of the coca plant - the same plant from which cocaine is made. Locals claim it helps with adjusting to the high altitude; it certainly was a stimulant, but not as strong as I had hoped.

As we rode slowly up the bumpy dirt road it seemed every man, woman and child stopped working in the fields to point at us and yell, "Gringo, Gringo, Gringo!" It was like they were afraid we would forget and wanted to remind us.

After they yelled this to exhaustion they would walk next to us and ask for a gift or a tip or more often say, "Gringo, give me money."

This put us in an awkward position, as it went against my belief that handing out money or gifts is not responsible tourism and damages the local culture.

When we politely declined to give them something, it was common for them to throw rocks at us in anger. We could do nothing except endure the assault until we were out of range. I asked myself, "Where did they learn to act like this?"

The answer soon came to me a few days later when we saw a tour bus pull up to a school in one small town. The kids ran out of class and the people from the bus handed out folders, pens and notebooks. They had their pictures taken with the kids and then left in a cloud of dust, without noticing the crying kids they had left behind who were not aggressive enough to push their way to the front of the crowd to receive their school supplies.

Tim crossing a dilapidated bridge.

Tim with the kids from Chino Tingo.

An upset schoolteacher explained to us afterwards that every few months, foreign tour groups in buses drove through handing out presents and money. He added that these groups were teaching the locals to beg and expect handouts from all strangers. He had asked the government to stop the tour buses from entering the area, but they had done nothing.

I suspected these foreigners were on a mission to make themselves feel better about their own wealth; but in the process, they were robbing these people of their dignity and reduced them to beggars. I feared they had done irreversible damage to these people and their culture.

Helping others is important; but as I learned in rural Peru, there is a right and wrong way to be charitable. I believe it is better to give donations directly to the schools or churches, and let them distribute what's needed to the community.

When we arrived in the small backwater village of Chino Tingo, I did not want to believe it was our destination for the night.

The first thing I noticed was the absence of blaring music, which meant there was no electricity. People walked through town leading burros laden with goods; pigs crossed the dirt street; chickens ran in and out of homes. The one motor vehicle in town was a Peruvian National Police car.

It seemed odd the police would be watching such a small village, but we later learned the national police were present in every village in this area because of threats by the Shining Path antigovernment group. The Shining Path had been active recently with violent protests and roadblocks, and the police were out to maintain control. We would soon come to experience first-hand Peru's political tensions.

Cindie and Fritz went to look at the only room in town and a group of kids gathered around me and my bike, curious. They lived a life without electricity, and that meant no television or radio. Even newspapers did not make it this far into the highlands; most could not read them if they did. No one could afford any of these things anyway. We were the entertainment.

To make them laugh, I pretended my bike was a motorcycle by standing over it and acting like I was turning the throttle while I made engine noises. It was not long before the kids also were pretending they had motorcycles and racing each other through town.

When Cindie came to get me a little girl asked her, "Can he come out to play later?"

Startled by the question, Cindie replied, "Maybe after dinner."

Cindie led me to our cheapest room ever, at five soles (US $1.45) for both of us. It was basic; no running water or electricity, worn-out blankets on the bed. We shared the community bathroom, out by the road, with the entire village. Cindie had investigated and declared it unusable.

It was like we were camping indoors, with Cindie preparing dinner on our camp stove by candlelight. Fortunately, both computer batteries were charged and the evening's entertainment consisted of answering email and working on the web site, which had gained quite a following.

After dinner, the three of us discussed our observation

Cindie getting a ride to the next town.

that something was wrong with the general mood of the locals that went beyond people throwing rocks at us or asking for money. There was something in the air, an underlying tension; people were irritable and stared at us suspiciously.

We got an early start the next morning. Thirty kilometers (18 miles) from our next town, Cindie felt sick and she made us stop every five kilometers (three miles) so she could get off the bike and go to the bathroom. She suffered from a bladder infection, and the rough roads made it worse. We pulled into a restaurant for lunch and when the owner saw a crowd of local kids gathering around us, he suggested we bring our bikes inside to avoid problems.

After Cindie returned from the outhouse she said she could not ride any farther. We flagged down a car full of women and kids going to a market a couple towns away. Cindie got

Locals at the Plaza in Chavanillo.

in; I helped the driver put her bike bags in the trunk and tie her bike on top. We made plans to meet in the next town, and then she was gone.

This was the first time I had ridden without Cindie since the beginning of our trip; I felt incomplete without her. Fritz and I rode together slowly uphill, out of town. A group of kids followed us for about two kilometers yelling, "Gringo, Gringo." They never seemed to get tired of that word.

Chavanillo looked like yet another rough backwater village. Security was deteriorating the farther we rode back into the countryside. I worried about Cindie; would she have trouble watching her belongings when the usual crowd gathered around?

When Fritz and I rode into town, to our amazement we saw Cindie strolling up the road with two Peruvian National

Police officers. She said the police saw her get out of the car and immediately came over to help her carry her bike and bags into the only hotel in town. I introduced myself and thanked both of them for protecting my wife.

Ernesto said, "Our job is done now that she is in the company of her husband," and they walked back to the police station.

Fritz and I pushed our bikes to the hotel, but had to stop at the bottom of the steps where a large crowd of boys gathered around and stood uncomfortably close. Fritz, who traveled light, carried his loaded bike up the stairs; my load was too heavy and I removed my bags from the bike so they could be carried separately. I politely asked two teenage boys to stop touching my bags and they pulled their hands away, but this did not last long. They continued pulling at my zippers out of defiance.

One of the boys had successfully inched open the zipper on my rear pannier. The teacher in me came out as I scolded him and threatened to march him home and explain his actions to his father. Another boy noticed my attention was occupied; he had my seat bag unzipped and my spare inner tube halfway out. I grabbed the tube out of his hand and told him to go away.

At that moment, Fritz and Cindie returned for my last bags. I bid the kids goodbye, picked up my bike and carried it up the stairs. Most of those boys were good, honest kids simply interested in a stranger from a foreign land. I wished I could have spent my time talking to them, but instead I had to concentrate on a few bad apples.

We changed clothes and went out for yet another dinner of white rice and rubbery chicken. This was the only food we could find in these small villages, and the lack of a variety was wearing us down; we both had lost weight and were feeling weak.

The next day Fritz was eager to ride and continued on alone; he had friends to meet in Lima, still many days away. Cindie felt sick and spent most of the day sleeping while I wrote on the computer.

While we were getting ready to go to dinner, we heard a big commotion on the street. From our window we saw a political protest; the two police officers we met were nowhere in sight. The people in the mob were angry and shouting threatening slogans about the government. We could see the situation was about to explode. This scared us so much we cooked ramen noodles in our room instead. Dinner wasn't great, but at least we were safe.

The crumbling adobe walls of our room had a high, rusted metal ceiling. In an attempt to make the unheated room warmer, the owner put a plastic sheet under the real roof. When we went to bed the night before, I had heard movement in the ceiling and thought it was birds.

Right before we went to bed, Cindie noticed it shaking and heard a kind of scampering noise. Then I heard her scream in fright.

I thought the protesters were breaking down the door, but in Cindie's opinion it was much worse.

"Tail, tail!" She pointed at the edge of the plastic sheet,

where it did not completely fit up against the wall.

At first I couldn't see anything, but she had our big knife and a flashlight in her hand, ready for battle. She shined the light on what she said was a tail and I said, "Cindie, that's too big to be a tail."

She said, "No, Tim, it IS. A large, hairy rat tail."

The light beam from the flashlight must have scared the rats; the ceiling came alive with the running of hundreds of little feet.

"Mr. Travis, get me out of this room right now."

I pointed out the window to the crowd of people who were breaking bottles and burning flags. "No way."

Cindie was in a panic and kept repeating, "What do we do Tim? What do we do?"

I thought for a moment and jokingly asked, "What would Indiana Jones do in this situation?"

Big mistake. She was in no mood for my silly jokes. I calmed her down and explained it was better to deal with the rats than run around town seeking out the hotel owner to ask about switching rooms. Rats we could deal with; they were probably in all the connected rooms anyway.

Cindie was frantic but agreed to my only idea. Her hands shook as we hung our belongings from nails high on the wall, where we thought rats could not possibly reach. This took some time, and it calmed Cindie down from the initial shock.

Then she asked, "Will they get in my bed during the night?"

I had to tell her something. I could not have my wife flip out anymore. We were stuck between rats and an angry mob. I told her that rats were not meat eaters and would not be interested in her, although I had no idea how rats acted or what they ate.

I said, "The rats cannot crawl up the slick wooden bed post, but they can crawl up the blankets." This at least sounded reasonable. We pulled up all the blankets hanging over the side of the bed.

Once the lights were turned off, the rats in the ceiling went wild. They ran all around the plastic sheet and made the ugliest scratching, scampering, and squeaking noises. Cindie said it was like living under a rat race track. I tried to distract her by talking about how Peruvians always had several skinny dogs running around, but never a cat; a cat would be fat and happy here.

It did not take long before she abandoned her own bed, crawled into my small single bed and curled up next to me. Neither of us slept much that night; we were up early and left as quickly as possible.

We climbed for several hours on a rough dirt road to a summit of 4,000 meters (13,120 feet). Our slow progress gave more people the opportunity yell things at us in Spanish: "Give me your bike," "Give me your helmet" and most of all, "Give me money."

When we did not deliver, the rock throwing started. Sometimes people threw large rocks with the intent to injure us. Luckily, they never made contact. Now I understood why the German cyclist in Huallanca called the people in this area

The long decent into Huanuco.

stupid; I would call them aggressive.

We made it through the rock showers to our final summit for the day, where we fought off a dozen sheep dogs in four different waves of attacks. We were lucky they came in waves; it gave us a few seconds to reload by harvesting more rocks off the ground. Our final relief from the dogs came with the speed of coasting down one of the longest continuous descents on a bicycle in my life. It was 54 kilometers (33 miles) straight down 2,200 meters (7,200 feet).

But, there was still one event that would make this day memorable.

As we rode down a dangerous section of road, a shear cliff with no guardrail on our left and a rock wall on our right, my front wheel slipped to the side. I had never crashed on a loaded touring bike before and when I fell, the weight of my

119

Tim just after his bike crash.

bike handled differently than an unloaded bike.

When I have crashed in the past, I've rolled. This reduces injury by sharing the impact over different parts of my body, which means no one place is seriously injured. But my loaded touring bike did not allow me to roll; it struck the ground with great force, and when the dust settled, my right knee was buried in the dirt under my weight and 40 kilograms (88 pounds) of gear.

I pushed the bike off and stood up. My bike tights were ripped open, my right knee was gushing blood and we were in the Peruvian backcountry, where medical facilities were crude.

Cindie has a weak stomach for trauma and has been known to faint at the sight of blood. I walked around to show her nothing was broken, but I could feel about a million little

120

rocks ground into my knee that would have to be dug out later. I had to wait until she was in a more stable environment and over the initial shock of my crash before I showed her the full extent of my injuries.

I wrapped my knee in a bandana and rode the remaining 46 kilometers (29 miles) to Huanuco. On the way my knee swelled; the rough dirt road caused a painful jiggle with every bump.

As we approached Huanuco we came to one of the police roadblocks that was becoming common in the area, but they usually waved us through. This time, they stopped us and sternly demanded to see our passports and asked us questions. "Where have you been?" "Have you seen anything suspicious?"

When they saw the dried blood on my leg an officer asked, "Who did that to you?"

"I had an accident. It was my fault."

Once they were satisfied with our story they said, "Someone was murdered on this road yesterday. Be careful in this part of Peru."

Our first thought was of Fritz, who rode through this area yesterday. I asked the police officer, "Was it a German cyclist?"

"No, he was Peruvian."

We were relieved somewhat, but eager to check email to see if Fritz had written us.

When we arrived in Huanuco, we quickly checked into a hotel. I took a shower and scrubbed the dried blood and

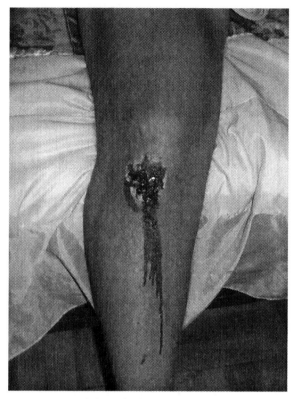

Tim's knee before he washed it.

rocks out of my swelled knee. I was ready to show Cindie my injury.

When she saw it, she screamed. "Where did all your skin go? I can see your bone."

I took a closer look and saw my wound was worse than I initially thought. My freshly cleaned knee had a noticeable absence of flesh about the diameter of a golf ball. When Cindie picked up my ripped tights to wash them, she found a thick flap of skin that used to belong to me.

We stayed in Huanuco for a week, waiting for my wound to stop bleeding and scab over. Cindie disinfected it and changed

Protest caught on video tape.

the dressing twice a day, even though she hated the sight of blood. After all the gauze, tape, and antibacterial cream were exhausted from the first aid kit, she was off to the pharmacy to buy more. I thought back to my younger solo years on the road and wondered how I survived without her.

One early Sunday morning during a walk around Huanuco we saw another heated political protest. The street vendors wanted to sell their wares from their carts in the Plaza de Armas, but the city recently banned them from the Plaza because it disrupted traffic. Hundreds of people marched in the plaza, chanting slogans and shouting demands to meet the governor.

Police officers showed up in riot gear, ran towards the growing crowd and randomly beat protestors with clubs. The beatings continued even after the victims were lying on the ground and begging them to stop. It was madness.

I thought the world should know about this brutal human rights violation. I turned on my video camera to capture a woman beaten by the police into a motionless state after she tapped a policeman's riot shield with her broomstick. As I filmed, the violence grew and moved in our direction. The police saw me filming and pointed at us. I knew they wanted my camera. Even though my knee was injured, we ran a couple blocks and ducked into an Internet cafe.

When we told the owner what we had just witnessed, he was not surprised; these kinds of protests were occurring more frequently, and the police were using more violence to deal with them. He accepted cops beating people as normal, which was as much of a shock to me as seeing the beatings themselves.

He described the general discontent and unrest among the rural population and stressed that something big was about to happen. We set out on this trip to learn about the world and have a bit of adventure, but "something big" sounded like more than we wanted to experience.

We left Huanuco before the growing political tension escalated out of control. I would have preferred to give my knee more time to heal, but instead I bandaged and wrapped it and continued riding.

The climb from Huanuco to Cerro de Pasco ascended 2,580 meters (8,500 feet) on smooth pavement and took us three days. The second night we stayed in a hotel; the owner said a German cyclist named Fritz had stayed there a week earlier. Just to be sure, I showed her a photo of Fritz on our camera

124

and she confirmed. We were relieved to know he was ok.

Twenty kilometers (12 miles) before Cerro de Pasco we pulled over at a combination mechanic's shop and store to buy snacks. A large truck full of noisy sheep was lifted up with a light jack meant for a car. Tools and empty beer bottles were scattered around. The oil pan was off, and dirty oil had been dumped into a ditch.

The mechanic must have been paid in beer; everyone involved was noticeably drunk. Two men under the truck were wrestling with the transmission while the rest were standing around. I feared the truck would fall off the jack at any minute and crush the men under it.

I heard a man under the truck ask another man, who was kicking an empty beer bottle, if the parking brake was on. He answered, "No, it will have to be fixed next."

The owner staggered over to the store, announced they were out of beer and would have to switch to whisky; nobody objected. He finally noticed us sitting in the warm sun as he entered the store. We greeted him, pointed at a bottle of water and a pack of crackers and asked, "How much?"

He claimed the bottle of water cost the equivalent of US $5 and the pack of crackers was even more. I told him the price I had paid in other stores and he countered with another inflated price. I restated the fair price, handed the water bottle and the crackers back to him and said, "No thanks."

Cindie and I had played this game several times before, and she knew what to do; we stood up and acted as if we were leaving. As I swung my leg over my bike he accepted my offered price. I paid him, made sure the transaction was complete, and then returned with our snacks to our seats in the sun.

The owner called the others over to meet us. As one of the men crawled out from under the truck, he accidentally kicked the flimsy jack. The truck shuddered and the sheep in the back became excited. I thought someone surely was going to die. Cindie muttered, "Oh no" and quickly looked away. But he stood up, dusted himself off and walked over, unconcerned.

The smelly, drunken men covered in motor oil gathered around us, and we had a friendly conversation about our bike trip and different places in Peru we had visited. One of them asked us for our address in the USA, probably because he thought it would help him get a work visa. While Cindie was explaining that we no longer had a permanent address, I overheard the other men discuss in Spanish how they were out of money and booze. They must have thought we did not understand them unless we were speaking face to face because they went on to say, "These gringos are rich, they have lots of money, they should buy us a bottle of whisky."

I heard them agree not to let us go until they received a large amount of money from us. I gave them the following address on a piece of paper:

Mick Jagger

99 Red Balloons Drive

Rocky Mountain Way, Arizona USA

8675309

As we were leaving, the owner directly asked me for money so they could buy whisky. I said, "My religion does not permit me to drink or buy booze."

Cindie gave me a puzzled look.

He asked, "What religion are you?"

"Jedi Knight."

I guess he had never seen the movie Star Wars.

He staggered closer to me as we mounted our bikes and asked for money again in a threatening tone.

I firmly said, "No."

The men removed their hands from their pockets and widened their stance.

I quickly made up a story and said, "We have to get going because a policeman, Jose in Cerro De Pasco, is expecting us. We met Jose a few weeks ago in Lima and he invited us to dinner at his house today. Isn't today Sunday?"

The owner replied, "Yes, today is Sunday."

I motioned to Cindie to get on her bike. "We better not be late, or he will come looking for us. Don't forget to write!"

Cindie gave me the "Don't overdo it, Mr. Travis" look and we rode safely away.

In the final kilometers before Cerro de Pasco, we saw our first herd of llamas, curious animals with long necks that twist and turn into the most expressive postures. They walked to the side of the road and stared at us as we passed.

Cindie slowed down to take a closer look and said, "I would love to bring one home."

"That would be some souvenir."

Cindie riding near a Llama.

Blizzard conditions in Cerro de Pasco.

Peru, Continued: A Bicycle Crash on a Dangerous Road

The city of Cerro De Pasco is a mining town and larger than we thought was possible at 4,380 meters (14,370 feet). The altitude made it cold and hard to breathe. The people who grew up here probably have hearts and lungs double the normal size. The miners were short, stocky and seemed to like sunlight as much as a vampire does.

It was snowing hard by the time we arrived at the town plaza and we were happy to be no longer riding; it was the wet slushy stuff that sticks and freezes to everything and makes cycling dangerous.

The bad weather did not stop a crowd of kids and interested adults from forming around us. They repeatedly asked if we rode our bicycles up the mountain from Huanuco. It was obvious they did not think it was possible.

We pushed our bikes into an old hotel lobby where the floor was wood and creaked with every step. Our room was unheated; the temperature hovered just above freezing. Heaters of any kind did not exist in this hotel, or in any other place we stayed in the Peruvian Andes.

Our bed had six wool blankets so heavy that when we crawled under, it was hard to breathe. It was odd to be able to see our breath in bed in a furnished hotel room; I bet we both looked like smoke stacks in our sleep.

This was the highest altitude we had ever slept. Cindie woke up in the middle of the night barely able to breathe; her chest felt tight and her heart was racing.

I sat up with her. To calm her down I said, "It's OK, everything is going to be all right," and eventually she went back to sleep.

The morning we planned to leave I grabbed a water bottle for a drink and found it was frozen solid. Outside the frosty window a full-scale blizzard was raging. We could not ride in this weather.

We both had developed altitude-induced headaches that aspirin could not cure. Cindie wanted to ride to a lower altitude where it was warmer and she could sleep better. She thought it was inhuman for anyone to live with no heat in a place this cold; even the toilet had ice floating in it.

Instead of leaving, we spent the morning in a bakery drinking coffee and eating empanadas, small meat and cheese pastries. In the afternoon we went to an Internet cafe, where everyone at the computers wore a thick wool hat and a heavy coat. They only removed their gloves for brief periods of typing. We received an email from Karen, a friend from Arizona; she would be arriving in Cusco in a couple weeks and we made plans to meet her.

The next day it was sunny and cold. We left Cerro De Pasco but did not escape the high altitude for a few more days. The sides of the road were blanketed by several inches of white snow. It was a pleasant change to be riding on flat, paved roads, and the scenery was vast and breathtaking. Trees did not grow at this altitude; we could see forever across the high valleys to uncountable snow-capped peaks. We occasionally encountered sheepherders and angry sheep dogs, but the flat road gave us the advantage of speed, which eased our escape.

At La Oroya we calculated we did not have enough time

130

Cathedral in the main plaza in Cusco.

to ride to Cusco if we wanted to meet Karen, so we took a bus. We arrived in Cusco an hour before sunrise and we reassembled our bikes in the morning moonlight. With taillights flashing, we rode cobblestone streets to the main plaza.

The ancient city of Cusco is a maze of tight twisting streets built long before the automobile existed. When we finally broke out of the manmade canyons and into the open space of the plaza, it was breathtaking. Two giant Catholic cathedrals dating back hundreds of years stood on either side; they were covered with sculptured art and oozed colonial history. All the other buildings surrounding the plaza were just as old and also boasted elaborate architecture. It felt like we were standing in a living, breathing museum. In the deserted early hours of the morning, we enjoyed a peaceful sunrise over Cusco.

Inca women with her llama.

With some searching, we found a hotel with hot water and electricity that was within our budget. It had been weeks since we had taken a shower that was not painfully cold. The toilet even had a toilet seat! We had entered civilization again. After a short but wonderful visit with Karen we spent our time repairing and cleaning our bikes and equipment, and exploring the city.

Cusco's historic charm draws cash-bearing tourists from all over the world, and the town is filled with shops and restaurants that cater to these relatively well off visitors. The upshot of this kind of development: We ate pizza, frequented salad bars and even saw Hollywood movies. We were surprised to find many business owners spoke English.

The down side was what I called "tourist pollution," which occurs when the tourist industry overwhelms the local culture and turns it into something less than authentic. In such places, foreign visitors cease to be human and are seen merely as a source of money. Around the central plaza, literally every few feet a restaurant employee shoved a menu in our faces and said in English, "You eat here. You like very mucho."

Kids followed us for blocks, insisting we buy postcards or mass-produced trinkets. Locals were not interested in chatting with us unless they could sell us something.

Other foreign travelers became a valuable source of local information. The political crisis in Bolivia was on everyone's mind, mainly because it affected travel plans; the indigenous farmers were angry with their U.S.-educated president for two reasons.

First, he allowed the U.S. military to spray their coca fields with herbicides that killed their crops and their livelihood. Coca leaves are intertwined with the local culture and centuries-old traditions. Rural Bolivian farmers cultivated coca leaves to make tea and chewed leaves to ward off hunger and fatigue.

Second, the Bolivian government had recently proposed a plan to export its natural gas reserves via a pipeline through Chile. Bolivia became a landlocked country when Chile took their seacoast and ports in a war over 150 years ago, and Bolivians were still angry about losing their land. Most did not like Chileans or want them to prosper from their gas reserves, the second largest in South America.

In protest of these issues, armed farmers closed off the borders with neighboring countries and blocked all roads

Machu Picchu.

A court yard near the Temple of Sun (circular building on the lower left).

into the capital city of La Paz. Tourists were prevented from entering the country; those who were unlucky enough to be in Bolivia before it was sealed off were trapped inside. Foreign governments were airlifting out their citizens. The country was no longer receiving food and goods, and La Paz had started to experience increasing shortages of everything from gasoline to bread.

Worst of all, the numerous clashes between those manning the roadblocks and the uniformed army were killing people daily. Several thousand striking miners marched into the capital with explosives, adding to the chaos and death toll. The protesters were demanding the current president leave the country and the gas plan be terminated.

Most travelers we spoke to were avoiding Bolivia and rerouting through Chile. Cindie and I did not want to miss visiting this fascinating country; we stayed in Cusco for two weeks waiting for the political turmoil to end.

During our stay in Cusco we visited the most famous tourist attraction in South America, the Incan ruins of Machu Picchu. The only way to get to Machu Picchu, other than walking, was by train, so we left our bikes with the hotel owner. The direct luxury train was expensive; we chose the cheaper option that included a bus, a mini van, and a short ride on a second-class train. The people we encountered on this route were local Peruvians and university students from all over South America. It felt like a pilgrimage of sorts.

Machu Picchu was built by an Incan ruler over six hundred years ago. The ruins sit at about 2,400 meters (7,900 feet) and include over two hundred buildings. Temples and residences

Llamas like this one, wander freely at Machu Picchu.

The terraces may have been used to grow corn.

were surrounded by terraces on which corn and potato crops were planted. Machu Picchu was abandoned before the arrival of the Spanish conquistador Pizarro and remained undiscovered until 1911, when a professor from Yale University, Hiram Bingham, found them.

We arrived early at the ruins - before the large crowds of tourists from the luxury train - and made our way to the highest point, called the Watchman's Hut, where we were treated with a breathtaking view of the surrounding area. The ruins are perched on a plateau high above a meandering river, and in the background jagged green peaks thrust through the morning mist. We explored the ruins the entire day and then walked to the nearby village of Agua Calientes. I took over two hundred pictures during our visit; that's a record for me and speaks to the amazement and beauty of the place. Later we would choose 60 of the best and post them on our web site.

We returned to Cusco and the news that the political crisis in Bolivia had plunged into chaos, with violent armed clashes growing worse. We tried to remain optimistic and made plans to ride towards the Bolivian border; if we ran out of time on our Peruvian visa and Bolivia was still in chaos, we would catch a bus to Chile.

My knee injury from my crash on the way into Huanuco finally scabbed over and no longer required bandages. It had taken a month for the wound to close up.

We pushed our loaded bikes into the central plaza for one last photo session. There we met Tony, from Canada; he was cycling from Lima to Argentina, and we exchanged emails.

Cindie stopping behind a herd of Alpacas.

Parade in the streets of Puno.

We did not know it at the time, but we would meet him again and ride together in Argentina. From Cusco we cycled through numerous small villages on an undulating rode until we eventually climbed to a high pass. From there we descended to the Altiplano, a vast high plateau in the middle of South America and spent several enjoyable riding days on our way to Puno, Peru.

One afternoon we caught up to a family moving a large herd of alpacas. The herd was scattered and the family was having trouble coaxing them off the dangerous road. When Cindie rode up to the herd, she was enlisted by the father to help move the alpacas. I hung back and filmed her yelling, "Get along little dogies!" at the alpacas while nudging them along with her bike. It was a thrilling experience with a different way of life.

Five days out of Cusco, the deep blue water of Lake Titicaca came into view; at 3,830 meters (12,600 feet), it is the highest navigable lake in the world and the minimum elevation of the Altiplano.

We arrived in Puno to see a parade of local musicians playing flutes and dancers in native dress. We stayed there a couple of days and took a boat to the floating islands of Uros in the middle of Lake Titicaca. The Uros are made of reeds growing in the shallow parts of the lake, and the indigenous people have constructed entire villages on these floating platforms. Everything is made of reeds, from the boats to the houses. It is an amphibious life, where even two-year-old children can swim and fish.

It was in Puno that we heard the wonderful news on our

Floating town of Los Uros.

. Fisherman in a boat made from reeds.

short wave radio: The controversial Bolivian president resigned and fled to Miami to live in exile. The interim president put the gas pipeline plan on hold and promised to hold elections in a few months.

The leader of the farmers called off the roadblocks and ended the general strike. He gave the new president an ultimatum: "Call off the army and hold elections within 90 days, or we strike again."

This seemed an impossible task given the amount of turmoil, but at least we had 90 days to visit Bolivia and get out before the deadline was up.

While in Puno, Cindie felt sick and thought she had a bladder infection; below she describes our trip to the hospital.

Tim and I went to the general hospital by taxi, and our Spanish was good enough to get through hospital admissions without too much of a hassle. I explained my symptoms in Spanish to the doctor assigned to me: Painful urination occurring frequently over the last three weeks. He requested a urine test and sent me downstairs to the laboratory.

When I arrived at the counter and asked for a sterile cup for my urine sample, they said they did not have any. A nurse walked quickly toward us shaking the last drops out of an empty glass Coke bottle. She handed it to me and said, "Use this for your urine sample."

I was dumbfounded. I could not believe a nurse in a city hospital wanted me to pee in an empty Coke bottle. I took it and went into a women's toilet that was so dirty I was afraid to touch anything. It was a harder task than I expected and while completely missing the mouth of the container at first, I thought, "How accurate can a urine test be when the sample comes from a Coke bottle?"

Finally, I had my specimen for the lab - now all I had to do was get it there. I was embarrassed to be walking down the hall with a Coke bottle full of what was obviously urine. I tried to hide it the best I could. The halls were crowded; at one point a woman slammed into my elbow and I almost lost my specimen all over the floor. With relief I handed my sample to the lab technician, who didn't seem surprised to see it was in a Coke bottle.

An hour and a half later, the results showed I had a bacterial infection. Tim joked that I also had high caffeine, sugar, and artificial color.

The doctor prescribed an antibiotic; Tim prescribed Sprite. The six-day dose of ciprofloxacin cost 2.9 soles (US $0.84). The hospital visit was a success and the antibiotic cured my bladder infection.

From Puno we made the two-day trip to the Bolivian border. We had mixed feelings about saying goodbye to Peru. We had spent three months there and were comfortable with the currency, customs, and Spanish accent. Peru had the most beautiful and striking scenery. It also had the most difficult and aggressive people of any country we had been in.

Chapter 6
Bolivia: Pickpockets in the City

Tim on the road to El Alto.

Cindie came out of the immigration office at the quiet border crossing in Peru and said the border official pulled out a calendar, counted 89 out of the allowed 90 days, and stamped our passports permitting us to exit the country. While waiting her turn, she saw a backpacker fined for overstaying her visa by 14 days and charged 60 soles (US $20) for each additional day; the woman did not have enough money and they took her to a back room. I appreciated Cindie staying on top of these things and realized I would have seen a lot of back rooms if I traveled without her.

The Bolivian side of the border was a couple hundred meters away. We rode over and Cindie returned from the

Crosses at the church in Copacabana.

immigration office and announced, "He wanted to give us a 30-day visa. I asked for a 90-day visa. He took a look outside at you and the bikes, changed his mind and stamped 90 days in our passports. We were lucky because the other tourists were only getting a 30-day visa!"

Shortly after crossing the border, we saw a disturbing

reminder of the previous weeks' turbulence. In a road cut through a small hill were boulders and a few burned out cars, which had been used to stop traffic. It was a logical place - on the highest point with several escape routes. If I were in charge of a group of angry farmers facing an organized army of trained and well-armed soldiers, I would have chosen the same place to defend.

The most depressing features of the abandoned roadblock were the spent bullets mixed with dried pools of blood. They told a sad story of a battle where the outcome was tragic for men on both sides of the conflict. My spine tingled.

In Copacabana, Cindie found a room for US $5 in what appeared to be the most expensive hotel in town. Our room came with a private bath, hot shower, toilet (with a toilet seat, which Cindie had come to think of this as a luxury) and an incredible view of Lake Titicaca.

In front of the large window overlooking the lake I set up the desk, arranged all my books, maps, and computer and worked dozens of hours writing the latest newsletter. I watched the sunset over the vast reflective lake every evening as I typed away. We stayed for a week.

One year earlier, in Ocosingo, Mexico, we experienced how rural Mexicans celebrated El Dia de los Muertos (Day of the Dead). Now we were in Copacabana, Bolivia, where this important holiday is called Dia de Todos Santos (All Saints' Day). The differences between how these two countries observed this same holiday were striking.

In southern Mexico it is a festive time, with large family picnics on the tombs of their ancestors and intoxicated

Mourners gather at graves in the cemetery.

Mourners in the cemetery.

men telling funny and entertaining stories about dead family members. Kites fill the air and children play hide and seek among the headstones in the cemetery.

In Bolivia, it is a somber occasion. As in Mexico, families gather at the cemetery with food; but they sing sad songs in a language other than Spanish to remember and grieve lost loved ones.

We knew from reading Peruvian newspapers that some of the most intense violence over the last few weeks centered in this area; now we were seeing firsthand the aftermath of recent clashes between protestors and the military. Mothers, sisters, and grandmothers in the brightly colored dresses of their indigenous clans cried uncontrollably around freshly dug graves. Fathers and brothers, hardened from years of conflict, promised the dead they would soon seek revenge for their youthful deaths. This vicious cycle of oppression, violence, and revenge seemingly had no end. We were moved by the violence and grief experienced by the locals and wished there was another way to solve the political problems of Bolivia.

The ride out of Copacabana and around the southern shore of Lake Titicaca had views of snow-capped mountains towering over the deep turquoise lake. The road was smooth and for the first time in many weeks, the wind was at our backs.

We stopped at a store, where a local family standing on the roadside told us they were waiting for a professional bicycle race called the Tour of Bolivia to pass. Occasionally, someone along the road had a small radio playing the coverage of the race and a crowd of 50 or so excited spectators huddled around

Cyclists waiting for the race to begin.

it. I asked a barefoot old man watching a herd of llamas what station the race was on and tuned into the coverage.

When we stopped for lunch, a crowd gathered around us to listen to the race blaring from the radio in my handlebar bag. The announcer spoke Spanish fast and he was hard to understand. I gathered that several reporters followed the race in cars and were transmitting updates to the announcer via cell phone. The race takes place over 18 days and this year featured professional cyclists from all over Latin America as well as a visiting Danish team.

Minutes before the final sprint, we rode into Tiquina and took our place among the spectators. We saw 200 racers in colorful uniforms covered in corporate sponsors come charging towards the finish line. At the last moment, a Colombian cyclist darted ahead of the pack and won the day .

Bolivia: Pickpockets in the City

After, we spoke to a bicycle mechanic working for the Bolivian team. He said the race would be ending in La Paz tomorrow; it would be a perfect day to ride into the capital, as the road would be closed to auto traffic. We decided to push on so we could make the capital the next day.

After a night in a hotel with a panoramic view of the Andes we left early, waited in El Alto for the police to close the road, and then descended into La Paz on a traffic-free four-lane highway.

The racers were only a half hour behind us. Cycling fans crowded the sides of the road, pushing and shoving to achieve the best view of the action. When they saw me flying down the steep hill with Cindie following behind, they thought we were part of the race - until they saw I had large bike bags and a tent strapped to my rack. The crowd cheered when I threw my arms in the air as if I had won the race, even though I was nowhere near the finish line.

Turning off the closed racecourse and into the congestion of a large South American city was a nasty return to reality. I suddenly awoke from my dream of winning the Tour of Bolivia.

Once again, I watched our bikes on the sidewalk while Cindie went in search of an affordable hotel room; but shortly after she left, I realized I had not secured our gear for this high-risk situation. Our camera and radio were still in my handlebar bag, valuable tools remained in my outside pannier pockets, and I was sitting in the middle of a tourist zone - home to pickpocket teams, bag slashers and con men.

I told myself repeatedly, "Don't take your eyes off the

149

Cindie pointing at the no bikes sign, well not today.

La Paz.

bikes. Don't take your eyes off the bikes." I wanted out of this dangerous-looking neighborhood and hoped Cindie would find a room quickly, regardless of the price.

Most people walked by going about their daily business. Then a cute old man leaning on a cane and dressed in a worn but clean suit stood slightly behind me and asked for directions. I continued to look at the bikes and could only see him in my peripheral vision. He had a map in his hand and wanted me to look at it. He asked me what street we were standing on. I refused to take my eyes off the bikes, even though I felt disrespectful for not turning and facing him when I spoke.

With my back to him I said, "I am a tourist and not familiar with the city."

He pleaded with me to help him find the location of his important doctor's appointment. He pointed at the map trying to divert my attention from the bikes and was upset when I would not help him.

Then a young man bumped into me, obscuring my view of the bikes with an open newspaper. I immediately knew something was wrong. I forcefully pushed him out of my way and he fell to the ground. With my view of the bikes restored, I saw a woman with her hand in my handlebar bag. I grabbed her and forcibly removed her hand from my bag.

At the same time, I yelled in Spanish, "Police! Help me! Thief!"

The woman skillfully broke free from my grip, the young man on the ground got up and the old man dropped his cane; they all ran in different directions. The street vendors around me covered their wares and took a defensive posture. An old woman selling onions and potatoes nearby warned me there would be more problems if I stayed longer.

Cindie returned to find me trembling with shock. I could think of nothing but getting out of there and said, "Get on your bike and ride."

She hesitated for a moment, and then realized something serious had happened and complied. We raced through traffic to a better part of the city with heavily armed "Tourist Police" standing on the corners. We pushed our bikes into a hotel lobby. I finally felt safe.

We were extra careful with our valuables while on the streets of La Paz that week. I wanted to take pictures of this interesting and historical city, but I never felt comfortable bringing our camera out of the room. This may have been overly paranoid; we never saw or heard of more crime, but I had learned to follow my instincts while traveling.

While in La Paz, Cindie once again bought souvenirs with plans to mail them home. Once she started shopping, there was no stopping her. She loved everything about shopping except the bargaining. That was my job, other than occasionally trying things on and carrying bags.

She bought Alpaca sweaters, a matching Alpaca hat and gloves, dozens of hand made finger puppets and who knows what else, but managed to spend only US $25 for everything. We stuffed her treasures into a box and shipped them to the States through the Bolivian postal system.

The ride out of La Paz was not nearly as fun. Instead of an

exciting, traffic-free plunge, my bike computer steadily read 0 kph as we grinded up a steep road busy with vehicles coughing thick black exhaust. I was suffering from flu symptoms - body aches, a stuffy head. The climb ended in the city of El Alto, where trash blowing in the streets obscured our vision.

Once we rode clear of the dense urban area, we pulled into a gas station to eat. I felt shaky and clammy; I told Cindie I couldn't go much further. In the wide-open spaces of the flat Altiplano, we easily found a suitable place to camp behind an abandoned building. We had an incredible view of a snow-capped mountain framed by a deep blue sky. It was wonderful to be away from the noise and pollution of the city; even the cold Andean nighttime temperatures did not prevent us from sleeping soundly. The next morning, I felt better and we continued on.

The extreme poverty of rural Bolivia became apparent when even sizable villages didn't have the most basic of stores or food stalls; eventually, we found an old woman willing to sell us stale bread. I was glad Cindie had stocked up on provisions in La Paz. It was disturbing that this area was even more impoverished than northern Peru.

We found a place to camp far off the road that night. High winds forced us into the tent early for warmth, spoiling the incredible sunset. Our water froze during the night; we awoke to a large herd of llamas and sheep walking around our tent the next morning. But the wind had stopped and the sun was warm; we dragged ourselves out of our comfortable sleeping bags, drank some coffee and got ready to start another day down the road.

Small villages on the Altiplano.

Young visitors to our campsite.

After the crumbling small villages of the Altiplano, the modern and youthful city of Oruro was a nice change of pace.

While I waited for Cindie to come back from her room search, three men in business suits and sunglasses, smelling of cheap aftershave, approached me. They displayed official looking ID and asked to see my passport. They were from Immigration, and were gruff and direct in their questioning.

Finding my passport was a problem; I told the official my wife was looking for a room and with a forced chuckle, said, "I am not sure where she keeps our passports, somewhere in her stuff; you know how it is, being married. If I make a mess of her bags she gets mad."

He looked down at me through his dark sunglasses and demanded, "Where did you cross the border into Bolivia?"

"Copacabana." I now was frantically digging through Cindie's panniers to find my passport and stalling him with the story of the bike race.

He cut me off and barked, "How many days have you been in Bolivia?"

I avoided answering; I hadn't kept track of the days. That was another one of Cindie's jobs. By this time I had completely gone through two of her four bags and had stuff piled high on park benches, but I didn't worry about thieves with these big thugs surrounding me.

I knew it was illegal for a foreigner to be without a passport in their possession. They could have easily taken me in or extorted a bribe from me if they wanted to; I could sense they were getting tired of dealing with me. I continued pulling Cindie's stuff out of her bags in a panic. The plaza started looking like a yard sale.

To this day, I believe the thing that saved me from bureaucratic disaster was the sight of four days' worth of Cindie's dirty laundry. As they were leaving, one of them told me we had one hour to report to the immigration office with our passports.

I threw Cindie's belongings back in her bags, hoping she wouldn't notice; and when she returned, she took one look at her bike and said, "Have you been in my bags?"

I explained about the intimidating immigration officials and how I had no choice but to search for the passports.

"Oops. I should have told you where they were; sorry about that."

"Maybe in the hotel room we can go through your bags again. Do you need absolutely everything I saw in there - like that big pair of scissors and the three bottles of lotion?"

"I'll tell you where the passports are, but keep your grubby hands off my stuff."

We went to the immigration office. I watched the bikes while Cindie went inside with our passports to straighten things out.

She returned and said, "It seems as though most foreign tourists overstay their 30-day visa, and when you told them we rode from Copacabana on bikes they thought it was impossible to get here in less than 30 days. But they saw we had used only two weeks of a 90-day visa, and they let me go."

A local women in a parade in Oruro.

Oruro was a university town; young adults comprised most of the population. This abundance of young people made for a festive atmosphere, with pizza joints, ice cream parlors, and Internet cafes. Cindie absolutely loved seeing several newly released Hollywood movies in the theater.

We received an email from Fritz, our German friend we

cycled with in Peru; he was also in town and looking for us. A few hours later Fritz was knocking on our door, and the three of us made plans to travel together again through the next remote section of Bolivia.

Leaving Oruro was the last time we saw modern conveniences for two weeks as we headed deeper into a sparsely populated area of southern Bolivia. On our route, we knew of only two locations that had small stores and shabby hotels that catered to truck drivers. The rest of the nights would be spent in our tent.

The first day out of Oruro, we rode for hours through open spaces with the occasional adobe village melting into the earth. We were ready to stop for the night but had not yet located a water source, which meant we had to ride on. We planned to collect water at the first sizable town on our map, but none materialized. A year ago, this would have scared us; but now we had grown accustomed to the idea that something would always come along. We knew the road would torment us at times, but would always take care of us in the end.

We rounded a bend and found a thermal hot spring with a developed bathhouse built around it. By the number of trucks parked in front, I initially thought it was some sort of brothel. Instead, we found men innocently soaking their tired bodies in the heavily mineralized spring. In the land of cold showers, the hot water was a treat.

We asked the owner of the bathhouse if we could camp behind the building; he said we could camp anywhere we liked and gave us drinking water from a spring further up the mountain. The water looked clean, but I filtered it anyway.

After we set up camp and made dinner, I looked out over the vastness of the Altiplano and watched as an impressive lightning storm attacked the ground several kilometers away. The sunsets in this empty part of the world seemed to last for days. I tried to capture the brilliance with my camera, but a picture could only show so much.

Soaking in thermal hot springs made for a good night's sleep in the freezing temperatures.

The next day we rode to a town with a hotel and learned there were worse accommodations than setting up our tent on the side of the road.

Camping in Bolivia.

Bike trolleys in the Plaza in Copacabana.

Chapter 7
Bolivia, Continued: Running from Political Violence

Camping on the Salar de Uyuni.

We rode into Challapata through a swirling wind comprised of tons of trash mixed with thick clouds of dust and filth. The sewer was a large ditch that ran through town; the smell was so awful we chose routes well away from it. Something was drastically wrong here. The people had numb expressions, as if they didn't care about the conditions they lived in; an air of depression seemed to engulf the town, and us as well.

The best hotel we could find was dismal. The owner said technically there was a hot shower, but the city's water only worked for a couple hours in the morning. After we moved into a small dusty room, he announced he could not find the key. My instincts told me things would disappear from an

Cindie asking directions to Quillacas.

Adobe mud homes on the Altiplano.

unlocked room, so I remained behind while Cindie and Fritz searched the few shops in town for food. They returned with stale bread and old chocolate bars.

Luckily, we were there only for the night; the three of us were excited to be heading to the world's largest salt lake, the Salar De Uyuni. At a base elevation of 3,500 meters (11,500 feet), this part of the Altiplano is a dry and cold desert.

Finding water for the next several days of riding was my biggest concern. The best map we found for this part of Bolivia was not at a scale necessary for backcountry expedition. Our map showed several villages along our route, but that was not a guarantee any type of settlement or water source actually existed. Vague email reports from other cyclists told of two fresh water sources at least a couple days' bicycle ride apart.

Cindie and I played it safe and carried a two-day supply of water on our bikes when we left Challapata - 11 liters, almost three gallons per day. I carried 16 liters (4.1 gallons); Cindie, six liters (1.5 gallons); Fritz also carried several liters of water and a couple of bottles of Coke. We were glad it was mostly flat terrain, as the extra weight of the water would have been hard to haul up mountains.

The paved main road heading south from Challapata turned to dirt a kilometer before entering Huari, after which we were to make a turn onto a road that would generally take us to the southwest. We came to a road, but it was little more than a scratch in the dirt and asked a man coming toward us on an old one-speed bicycle if it was the road to Quillacas. He assured us it was, but added that Quillacas was far away.

Cindie standing in front of an adobe brick home.

Cindie and Fritz on the road to Quillacas.

Taking this road turned out to be an adventure; hours later, we realized it was the wrong turn.

We crossed a wide, flat plain with mountains in the distance, occasionally passing settlements that were little more than groups of mud houses protecting the inhabitants from the harsh, high-altitude climate. The only way to make a living is by herding llamas and sheep, which looked neither easy nor lucrative. Water is collected from shallow open holes in the ground; electricity is nonexistent.

The only sound came from the persistent howling of a cold wind. There was not even the familiar trash blowing around; people who produced everything they owned had nothing to throw away.

We came to several forks in the road, but could not locate ourselves on the map. We asked llama herders for directions, only to received confusing answers; they did not bother with roads. Eventually we had to trust the digital compass built into my watch. After a few hours our dirt track dwindled to little more than a footpath, which we hoped would continue southwest to some kind of landmark. It was now obvious this was not the road we were looking for on our map. We were lost. Only the llamas knew where we were, and they weren't talking.

We were relieved when our faint trail eventually intersected a more established dirt road - the road we had been looking for! Rising in front of us was a lone mountain and after several kilometers, our new road climbed steeply up its slope. At the top was the first village on our map, Quillacas, with one store and a single water tap next to the church. We

The main street through Quillacas.

Our campsite on the vast Altiplano.

waited for an indigenous woman to fill an old two-liter pop bottle with water before we topped off our own bottles.

We left town, coasted down a hill back to the barren plain and found a comfortable place to camp. When I looked towards the setting sun, I could not see anything built or even touched by humans. At these special moments, I am reminded that camping not only saves money - it brings us closer to our natural surroundings. I bid the world good night and slept like a rock.

In our travels I have learned not to expect every day to be a lovely spin through the countryside, even though most days are exactly that. The next day was tough - the endless kilometers of dirt road were either bone-rattling washboard (corrugated) or so sandy we had to push our heavy bikes for hours - but it was part of traveling this way.

However, it was towards the end of the day my real misery began. First, my tire went flat. On a loaded touring bike, this frustration is compounded by having to remove most of the gear before I can repair the flat.

Only a few kilometers later on a steep, sandy section of the road, my chain broke. Bike chains have a devious sense of timing and break at the worst possible moments. Repairing it is a dirty job and my hands turned black with grease. The water we carried could not be wasted on cleaning my hands, so I wiped them on my bike shorts when Cindie wasn't looking. Some things, she does not need to know about.

The most difficult times of this journey are when unexpected things go wrong. On this day, the road conditions and my mechanical problems only added to the real hardship that

Tim getting help collecting water from a well.

Cindie pushing her bike through the sand.

would unfold.

We arrived at Tambo Tambillo, the second of three villages on our route, late in the day. We needed to collect water and look for a place to buy food, but like so much of rural Bolivia, commerce was virtually nonexistent. The buildings were made of adobe, looked drafty, and probably leaked in the rare rainstorm. Several young kids met us on the edge of the village and we asked them where we could find water. They excitedly asked us to follow them and we formed our own little parade through their village.

We stopped at a newly built well with a hand pump and an engraving by an aid group in the concrete base. The kids wanted to pump the water, so I held out our water bag and at least ten little hands worked the pump. The water must have been deep, because progress was slow. Several times, I felt little fingers gently touching my hair. One of their mothers standing nearby told me the kids had never seen curly hair or white skin before.

Pointing at a large llama grazing in a makeshift soccer field, one little boy asked me, "Can you carry more on your bike than that llama?"

I said, "I don't know, I have never traveled with a packed llama before."

I could see by the look on his face that he didn't believe me. For these kids, packing a llama was part of everyday life. I tried to imagine what their lives were like without electricity, mass media or crime.

I stood up from tying the water bag onto my bike and felt

---

a muscle pull in my lower back. It was a sharp pain from deep inside. Suddenly, I could no longer support my own weight and had to lean on my bike.

At first I thought the pain would pass, but I quickly realized I was seriously injured. Although I could not stand, I was able to ride because the bike seat and handlebars supported most of my weight. But even this position was not comfortable for long because of the excruciating pain in my lower back.

Just outside the village, a cemetery offered a flat place to camp and we pulled over. Cindie set her bike aside and had to help me get off mine. Using the bike as a crutch, I tried to walk a few steps but the pain shot through my back and I fell to the ground. Cindie grabbed my heavy bike and rolled it safely to the side before it crashed on top of me.

The place in the dirt where I fell was where I remained for hours. Cindie and Fritz pitched the tent, cooked dinner and somehow helped me crawl into bed. That night I tossed and turned, unable to escape the persistent pain.

I felt slightly better the next morning when Cindie, Fritz and I discussed our options over breakfast. I wanted to try riding my bike; we were on a remote road with only three or four vehicles going by each day, and it would be a long wait for a ride. Cindie was flatly against me riding because she worried I would risk further injury to my back.

I took several more aspirin than the recommended dosage and hoped it would kick in quickly. We loaded the bikes, with Cindie and Fritz lifting anything heavier than a full water bottle. I had Cindie believing we were waiting for a ride until I forced my leg over my bike and started down the road.

170

Bolivia, Continued: Running From Political Violence

It was far from an enjoyable ride; every bump on that dirt road was painful, but the worst was getting off the bike and pushing through the sand. I ate aspirin like they were candy all day long.

We made it to Salinas, the last village on our route to the Salar that offered lodging. We found the hotel with the help of an old man on a bicycle while dodging huge rocks and burro dung in the road. The woman who ran the place boasted that her house was one of the few that had electricity and a refrigerator. She also claimed she had a hot shower; that turned out to be false.

A couple of solar panels and old car batteries ran a few dim lights, a shortwave radio, and a small black and white TV; people from the village stood in the doorway to catch a fuzzy glimpse of a soccer game. The refrigerator looked new, ran off propane, and was reportedly the only one within hundreds of kilometers.

We stayed two nights. I spent my time lying on my back in bed, typing a newsletter. The solar panel/car battery setup did not provide enough electricity to power my computer, so I ran the seven-hour battery down. The only activities I got up for were eating, going to the bathroom and cleaning up.

One night after dinner, I realized I had accidentally left our guidebook in the restaurant a few minutes after we returned to our room. When we went back, the owner said she saw a group of men leave with it. I asked where they went; she said they were far away, maybe we could find them in the morning. I knew this was unlikely, since they had just left and I had not heard a car start.

An obnoxious drunk man decided to get involved. He told us in Spanish he could speak English, but he only knew three words - "Me speaky English" - and kept repeating those three words in an attempt to show off.

I announced loudly enough for everyone to hear, "I will give the first person who returns my book 10 Bolivianos (the price of about three bottles of beer)."

I saw the restaurant owner whisper something to another man, who then disappeared. Not more than 30 seconds later the man returned with our book. The owner reminded me of the money I promised.

"I can see how you could have easily mistaken this big purple book written in English as yours and walk out with it."

I slowly searched for the money and handed it to the man; he looked down at the floor as he grabbed the notes. I held them long enough for him to look into my eyes and know that I was aware he was scamming me. As we walked out, I turned around to see the man and the restaurant owner splitting the money.

The promised hot shower never materialized, but this was no surprise as lodging owners we had recently come across were fond of stretching the truth. In fact, the water tap in the shower did not work at all. We were grungy from several days of camping without a shower, wanted to clean up, and resorted to using our solar shower. Cindie filled our water bag and laid it in the sun, which was strong at this altitude and latitude; a few hours later, the water was steaming hot.

The restaurant cook watched Cindie test the water with great interest. Cindie poured a little hot water on the cook's hand, and she called over her sisters, aunts, and daughters to feel the soothing water. Once we attached the showerhead and tied the bag full of hot water to the shower, the women understood how it worked. Cindie grabbed her towel, disappeared, and several minutes later emerged completely clean. The women discussed how to construct their own solar shower.

The night before we left Salinas, Fritz, Cindie and I debated how much water we should carry. We were not sure what was ahead; our map showed a large white space labeled "Salar De Uyuni" with no other information. We knew from our guidebook that tourists took Jeep tours from the other side of the giant salt flat to a restaurant on an island somewhere in the middle. We were counting on this island to have a fresh water source.

Cindie said, "If all goes well we can carry less water, because it's possible to ride the remaining dirt road to the salt flat, navigate across it, and reach the island with the restaurant in a single day."

I said, "That is a tempting scenario, but the key phrase is, 'if all goes well.' You know this never happens. It seems there are always glitches anytime we stray deep into the unknown. Tomorrow is full of unknowns - like getting lost on the way to the salt lake or the island 'somewhere in the middle.'"

Fritz joined Cindie in her opinion that carrying less water would be faster and made the island easier to reach.

I voted to play it safe, carry a full two-day water supply,

Cindie getting directions to the Salar from the man leaving the church.

The Salar de Uyuni in the background our road is on the left.

and have the option of camping along the way. To boost my argument I recited a long list of experiences:

"Do you remember the time in Arizona when I insisted we carry extra water and then later in the day a headwind cut our miles in half, and we had to unexpectedly camp in the desert? Remember in Mexico I insisted we carry emergency food, and a few weeks later we got caught in bad weather and had something to eat while we waited it out in the tent?"

Cindie realized we were better safe than sorry, and convinced Fritz to fill all our water containers.

We drew a crowd of curious but shy onlookers who watched us assemble the gear on our bikes in the early morning light. From the bewildered expressions on their faces, it was obvious they did not get many foreign visitors in their village.

We were never sure if we took the correct turns until we reached the last village, from which we could see the vast salt flat - an endless, solid white ocean.

We could not see the island, and there were no signs for which way to go. We stopped in front of the village church and studied our worthless map. A man walked out of the church and we asked him how to find the island. He said many things that were hard to understand, including something about wind direction and the flight patterns of some kind of bird. Finally, he told us to head toward the middle of two distant peaks; the island would be before these mountains and a bit to the left.

This sounded vague. I asked him if we should head

Riding on the Salar.

Camping on the Salar.

south-southwest. He looked up at the sun, put his hand out to make a shadow on the ground, thought for a few seconds, and answered an optimistic, "Yes!"

I asked him if there were any other villages out there or a place we could find fresh water. He laughed hysterically and said, "Salt! There is only salt, my friend."

Who needs a GPS when you have directions like this?

When the dirt road ended and the rattling of our bikes and gear stopped, we were delighted. We only noticed how irritating this constant noise was after it was gone. It was eerie how quiet everything became.

We entered the hard and perfectly flat surface of the salt lake, like the smoothest, biggest parking lot on earth. I never thought a place could be so beautiful and yet so empty at the same time - a wilderness of nothingness.

We zigged and zagged and played around on our bikes in this strange new environment. We stopped and took several pictures, then rode on. I checked my compass often; I knew we could easily get hopelessly lost on this endless salt ocean. It was more like navigating a boat than a bike.

After a few hours we could see a speck barely peeking above the horizon. We hoped this was our island. It was getting late; if we pushed on we could probably have made it to the island before dark, but we had plenty of water on board. I thought it would be fun to camp in the middle of the salt flat anyway, and Cindie and Fritz agreed.

The problem was picking a place to camp. Usually campsites are rare because of the lack of secluded flat places. On the

Tim having a cup of coffee early in the morning.

Tim's tire is completely ruined, boy am I glad we had a spare.

Salar, we had the opposite problem; everywhere was perfectly flat and secluded. After months of struggling to find suitable places to camp, we were dumbfounded by indecision.

"We can stop anywhere we like!" "OK, maybe a little farther." "How about here?" "Maybe over there?"

I finally squeezed my brakes and said, "Here!"

The sunset that evening was spectacular, and brought back memories of the beach in Southern California. As the big burning ball sank slowly into a sea of white salt, the strange surface turned a different color; first orange, then slowly turning darker into a bright red; then as darkness came, the color of deep red wine.

The next morning, I crawled out of my sleeping bag extra early and made coffee in the nearly freezing air. I wanted to sit in silence and watch the sunrise over this empty world.

When Cindie and Fritz woke up, I discovered my bike had yet another flat and went through the process of repairing it. I was not going to let this little problem ruin the grand experience of these unique surroundings.

A few minutes after I pumped the tire we heard a loud explosion; the sidewall of my tire had blown out.

"Great, this tire is now trash and I don't even have a trashcan to dump it in," I said angrily. The flat did not ruin the moment, but a completely ruined tire certainly did.

Luckily, I had been carrying an emergency spare tire with us since we left Arizona. If we had not had it we would have been in big trouble, as the island was still hours away by bike. I strapped the dead tire on the back of my bike so I could

Tim and Cindie on Isla (Island) Incahuasi.

The Salt Hotel where everything was made of salt including the beds.

dispose of it properly.

As we approached the island, we saw several Jeeps and foreign tourists buzzing around. Ironically, the beautiful salt flat now had black lines of exhaust from these vehicles used for these package ecotours. I was glad they only drove on the southern end of the salt flat; our arrival from the north let us experience the endless whiteness without the damage from the ecotours.

We were happy to find the island had water and places to camp. That evening we saw a Jeep pull in with two touring bikes tied on top. The cyclists, Martin and Iskasun, caught a ride from Chile because the dirt road was rough. They said they were from "the country of Basque" and spoke French, Spanish, and Basque.

I have never been to Europe and asked Martin, "Where exactly is the country of Basque?"

"It is between France and Spain and contains part of the Pyrenees Mountains." He went on to name several internationally famous professional cyclists who were Basques.

From the geographic description and the names of the famous cyclists, I gathered Basque is part of Spain in the same way that Texas is part of the U.S. I said, "Oh, so, you are from Spain?"

Apparently, this was the wrong thing to say. Everything stopped.

They explained what it meant to be Basque by way of a quick geography and history lesson. Martin said that a long time ago the Basque people came from Eastern Europe and settled on both sides of the Pyrenees, where maps now show France and Spain. The Basques speak a unique language, different from Spanish. The people on the French side of the Basque country are content with their official status as being French citizens, but many Basques living in Spain did not like to consider themselves Spanish citizens.

The next day Fritz, Cindie, Martin, Iskasun and I left the island together and rode toward the town of Uyuni, where all the Jeep tours started. We could have made it in one long day, but the thought of leaving this area so soon made me feel rushed; I wanted to experience another dazzling sunset and tranquil morning. I talked everyone into breaking the day in half and camping one more night near the famous salt hotel. The hotel is built with blocks of compressed salt, so the walls, seats, tables, and even beds are made of salt.

For me, taking the time to learn as much as I could from my travels was more important than drawing a longer line on a map. Memories of hours in the saddle faded, but rich experiences last a lifetime. I told them, "I don't want the riding to ruin my bike tour."

Nevertheless, we were relieved to reach Uyuni and civilization the next day. Cindie and Iskasun found a cheap, comfortable hotel with reliable electricity and a hot shower. We spent nearly a week there washing off road dirt and salt from our bodies, clothes and gear. Uyuni also had slow but consistent Internet, and I spent several hours posting pictures and answering email.

Unfortunately, we were all parting ways in Uyuni. Our new friends Martin and Iskasun wanted to keep moving north; they had already been to Argentina and Chile. We wished they were going south with us; they were an interesting couple from a part of the world we knew nothing about. Fritz wanted to take the dirt road to Chile and was running out of time; he would be sadly missed. It was hard to say goodbye to our traveling companions.

The day after they all left Uyuni, Bolivia's political tensions caught up with us. Large groups of miners on strike marched in the streets, lighting sticks of dynamite to draw attention to their cause. Protestors stopped all transportation in and out of town, including buses and trains. We heard it was not safe to leave on our bikes. We worried about our traveling companions and hoped they had left the area before the roads were blocked.

During the numerous unannounced street marches, the protesters demanded that businesses close. One evening we ate in a restaurant down the street from where a large protest march formed. The owner's family quickly turned off the music and lights, shut and locked the doors, and pleaded with the customers not to make a sound until the street cleared.

The Bolivian customers knew what was at stake and were obviously frightened and dead silent. This scared me so much I looked for the back door and formulated our escape plan. But the protesters passed, and the restaurant slowly came back to life.

Cindie and I agreed the stability of the area was deteriorating. We had to leave town soon.

A rumor circulated that there was a break in the negotiations and the protesters were allowing one train to leave town. Cindie made repeated trips to the train station to see if the rumor was true, but received a different answer every time. On one of her visits they were temporarily selling tickets for a single overnight train; Cindie's instincts and persistence paid off, and she bought two without hesitation.

With tickets in hand, she ran back to our room and said, "We have one shot to get out of this town."

We packed and quickly returned to the station. Hysterical people with no tickets now crowded the gate in a desperate attempt to board the train any way they could.

The train finally arrived; we rolled our loaded bikes through the checkpoints, put them in the baggage car and gratefully boarded the train. Through the window, we saw the situation growing out of control. The police were stopping people at gunpoint from climbing the fence.

Rumors flew through the train car that protesters would not allow the train to leave. An old woman sitting next to us silently clutched her rosary beads and prayed.

Finally, the scared conductor shut the door and the train rolled down the tracks. It was almost midnight. Everyone sat silently and looked out the window for any sign of trouble. The conductor did not check our tickets right away, but instead nervously looked out one side of the train and then the other.

Cindie quietly asked me, "What is he looking for? What does he know that we don't? What is our plan if there's trouble?"

I replied, "If there is trouble we go through the hatch above us to the roof."

Cindie was not too keen on that idea.

After an hour of expecting the worst, the conductor relaxed and went about his business of checking tickets.

In the morning, we arrived at the border between Argentina and Bolivia. We stayed on the Bolivian side for a couple days and made preparations to cross the border and start a new adventure in Argentina.

Boats on Lake Titicaca.

Fritz and Cindie on the way to the Salar.

Camping on the wide open Salar.

Chapter 8
Argentina: Traveling as an American During Wartime.

Crossing the border into Argentina.

The border crossing was relaxed, with a quick stamp out of Bolivia and a standard 90-day stamp into Argentina. A steady stream of Argentineans crossed into Bolivia to buy imported goods, avoiding the higher taxes paid on the same goods in Argentina - shoes made in China, portable electronics made in Taiwan, and computer equipment made in Europe.

While riding through the border town of La Quiaca, Argentina, Cindie yelled, "STOP!"

I slammed on my brakes. "What's wrong?"

"The light turned red." I looked up and noticed a traffic light over the intersection.

Peru and Bolivia seldom had traffic lights, and when they

Our last campsite on the Altiplano.

did, no one paid attention to them. This was not the case in Argentina, where cars stopped at red lights and more or less stayed within the painted lane markings, which I had almost forgotten about.

Drivers also used turn signals and honked less, which meant we had to revert to a more civilized style of riding. We used hand signals to indicate turns instead of whistling or making eye contact. The orderliness of the traffic was welcome, even if it meant the roads were more congested; Argentina had a large middle class that could afford new and used cars.

After withdrawing local currency from a busy bank machine, we were eager to ride deeper into this new country. The first few hours spinning on the flat road were enjoyable. With Cindie drafting a couple inches off my rear wheel, we made good time. We were approaching the Altiplano's southern boundary; soon this unique area above 3,500 meters (11,500 feet) would be relegated to memory. We wanted to camp one more night in the vastness we had grown to love.

We entered a village to pick up our usual overnight supply of water and noticed a tower. Cindie had worked with water systems in Arizona; evaluating the various pipes and pumps on the side of the road, she said, "The water system in this village is modern and well maintained. We can probably drink straight from the tap." This was something I had not heard since we had ridden through Costa Rica.

We stopped in the plaza for a rest and a US $0.15 ice cream. School had ended for the day and we watched kids in their uniforms fill their plastic water bottles straight from the tap and drink. It was time to take the test.

Passing would mean not getting sick, and not hand pumping water through our filter every day; failing would mean hours of abdominal pain and a trip to the pharmacy for antibiotics. I nervously stuck a water bottle under the tap, filled it, smiled at Cindie, and took a big drink.

She took the bottle from me and did the same. She noted, "This water tastes chlorinated. That's a good sign."

We both knew time would tell if the water was clean. I filled our bottles and our 10-liter water bag for camping. Even though Cindie acted confident the water was safe, she unnerved me when she bought a big pack of toilet paper on our way out of town.

We rode a few kilometers until we were well out of sight of

189

Leaving Tres Cruces.

any dwelling and made camp in an open spot with sweeping views of the Altiplano.

In the middle of the night I was awakened by a large truck squealing to a stop on the road near our tent. I grabbed my knife, pepper spray and flashlight and quickly unzipped the tent door.

I looked out and saw a truck driver urinating on his tire. He did not see our tent and bikes, even though there was a bright full moon. Knowing he was harmless, I zipped the tent door closed and was back in my warm sleeping bag before I heard the truck door slam shut and the large engine wind out first gear.

Cindie woke up and asked, "What was that, Tim?"

"Oh, nothing - go back to sleep."

Argentina: Traveling as an American During Wartime

Sometimes I feel like the family watchdog, listening for trouble while half asleep.

The next day at Tres Cruces we were stopped by immigration officers looking through everyone's luggage for who knows what. When it was our turn, a man in a uniform asked for our passports. Cindie rummaged through her bag and handed them over.

He said, "So you are from the United States. I have a brother who lives in New Jersey. He is always asking me to come visit. Do you think I would have trouble entering the USA?"

This was a loaded question. I thought carefully about my situation: I was at an immigration checkpoint wanting to be waved into this man's country without any delays or scrutiny; he was asking me how he would be treated at the border of my country. I could not tell him the truth, which was that a U.S. immigration official would want to see proof he had thousands of dollars in a bank account and an airline ticket out of the country, and would probably ask dozens of additional questions that might last hours.

Instead of answering him, I was silent.

He slapped me on my back and said, "Well, I can always sneak in like my brother did 15 years ago." He then lifted the gate and waved us through.

After clearing this final checkpoint, we entered a scenic stretch of highway where the Altiplano ended and rode downhill for two days. The entire drop was 3,000 meters (9,900 feet) and raised the air temperature, humidity, and oxygen content considerably. We started at the top of a small canyon

Standing near a cactus in northern Argentina.

Riding in northern Argentina.

and watched it gradually grow to monstrous proportions as we traveled down its path.

Strange formations of red and yellow rocks greeted us at every twist of the road, which Cindie explained were caused by folding, uplifting, and faults. I took long video shots of the sheer beauty while silently flying down the canyon.

Filming on the bike always scares Cindie; she is worried about the combination of my handling a bike at high speeds, being aware of traffic and looking through a camera. I am of the opinion it is worth the risk to capture the image of cycling through a unique place in the world. If only I could have filmed while riding through a large, unorganized city in Peru! Capturing the memory of chaotic traffic while dodging large trucks, aggressive buses, reckless taxis, slow burros, passed out men and the occasional chicken was impossible. Besides the high probability of getting the camera stolen out of my hand, I would surely crash or be hit.

Filming is relegated to perfectly smooth roads with little traffic; even then, on many recordings the microphone picks up Cindie screaming, "Mr. Travis, get your eye out of the camera and slow down!"

The last downhill stretch started in the familiar brown desert and in the blink of an eye, the landscape changed to a lush green world full of water and leafy vegetation. Cold and dry was now hot and humid.

When the road finally leveled out at the bottom, we stopped to change into our summer apparel. Our bodies were not used to the new climate; unused sweat glands had to get back in shape.

Camping on the grass for the first time in a long time.

The most welcome change was the oxygenated air. After months of acclimating to thin air, we were now flying along supercharged with the one thing every cyclist craves - oxygen. After a long day of riding, neither one of us felt tired.

We found a crowded campground with a busy pool. It was Saturday; people were off work and ready to party. Argentineans love to go camping with their families and stay up all night talking and drinking. We found a spot next to a large group that worked together in an accounting office. The kids were at the swimming pool, the women were cooking dinner, and the men were drinking wine and discussing politics and football (soccer).

As I was locking our bikes to a picnic table, I overheard their conversation. I did not know the names of any sports stars or politicians in Argentina, so I was confused about which subject they were discussing. At one point, I thought I heard one of them say the mayor of Buenos Aires scored two goals in one game. When they talked, they passionately emphasized their point with hand gestures and if it was important enough, these movements grew in animation to include both arms and their entire body.

Cindie bought beer and snacks from the campground store while I set the tent up on cut grass - something we had not done since the cornfields of Mexico well over a year earlier. I found an electrical outlet and began charging the computer so I could get some writing done. It was a relief to see the green charging light glow on the computer; electricity was hard to find when we free camped.

Just as I started typing, we were invited to our neighbor's campsite for wine and cheese. Writing my newsletter was important, but I could not pass up a party with locals. They were a little tipsy and their slurred Spanish was difficult to understand.

My new friend Vicente said, "What are you doing on a computer in a campground?"

"I am writing."

"This is a time for relaxing! No work is allowed."

He turned up the music and refilled my glass with wine. How could I argue? We did not talk about work the rest of the evening, but stayed up past our normal bedtimes discussing life.

Spending time with these Argentineans taught me about life's priorities; they take the time to enjoy each moment of

Riding Route 9 to Salta.

Horses running free on the outside of the fence.

the day. Sitting down for a meal is a special occasion, a time to relax and enjoy the company of family and friends. I could never picture them ordering food at a drive-thru and eating it in a car.

In my country, it is all too common to cram food in your face just to keep from feeling hungry. We are the inventors and masters of the fast food culture. I bet Argentineans have far less stress and stress-related illness than in the U.S. I liked their attitude, and their lifestyle; they believe enjoyment should not be something saved for the weekend or retirement.

Before we caught on to the sacredness of mealtime, we would stop for a rest in front of a little store, buy a couple bottles of pop and some cookies and sit on a rock or log, sipping our drinks out of the bottle and eating the cookies from the package.

This was an outrage to the Argentineans who witnessed it. More than one distressed store owner insisted we sit in a proper chair at a table, and occasionally even provided a fresh tablecloth. Two glasses appeared for our drinks and a plate for our cookies. Drinking out of the bottle was not proper. We quickly learned to enjoy life as the Argentineans did, and our breaks became more than just time off the bike.

Route 9 to Salta was narrow and almost traffic-free. It climbed over a small mountain range, but the modern road never became very steep. The air was fresh from the millions of thriving plants. Herds of wild horses wandered freely in their personal wilderness, their days filled with playing in the trees or eating the endless supply of grass. Often they

The Cathedral in Salta, Argentina.

did not hear our silent approach until we were upon them. Once they saw us, they took off running in a show of power and grace. Such freedom was a thing to protect. I wished this mountain road would go on forever; but after several climbs, we descended into Salta.

Salta was our first glimpse at urban Argentina and had everything you would expect in a modern city, with an extra dose of shopping and nightlife. It was on the international tourist trail and we were in the mood to socialize; we chose the most popular hostel from our guidebook.

Most of the backpackers had come to Salta by bus from

places that would have taken us three weeks to ride, but took them about 20 hours. We met travelers from all over the developed world: South Africa, New Zealand, Australia, Israel, Canada, Japan, and every country in Europe.

Ireland, a country of some four million inhabitants, had several people staying in the hostel. In contrast, the U.S. has about three hundred million citizens and only Cindie and me as ambassadors. We wished more Americans would take the opportunity to travel outside of the U.S.

An international news channel played in English all day on the satellite TV in the hostel's common area. We had not seen images from the news for several months while traveling in rural South America; we kept up on world events by listening to our shortwave radio. The footage coming in from Iraq was particularly disturbing, but added a necessary context to what we had heard on the radio.

The constant reporting from the battle lines in Iraq sparked discussion among the international guests. A young man who knew our nationality asked us, "What do Americans think about the war in Iraq? How long do you think the war will last?"

About a dozen backpackers gathered around to hear our answer. Cindie tried to explain we had been out of the U.S. since before the buildup and start of the war, so we could not accurately speak for the mood of the nation or reasons for the war.

Before Cindie could get this point across, another young woman put her guidebook down and angrily added, "Why do you Americans think you can always get what you want with bombs and guns? Why did you start the war in Iraq when the United Nations voted against it?"

I jumped in and replied, "I have neither a gun or bomb with me and I personally did not start a war. It's not fair to lump all Americans together with your generalizations."

A man sitting at a table who was visibly agitated pointed his trembling finger at me and said loudly, "No offense, but everyone knows Americans are so lazy that you would rather start a war so you can keep driving your cars instead of walking two blocks to the McDonald's." Several bystanders nodded their heads in agreement.

Thankfully, another listener spoke up and defended us.

"Did you know Tim and Cindie have been riding their bikes through South America? This neither burns oil nor can be considered lazy. They are proof your stereotypes do not work for all Americans. I live just over the border in Ontario, Canada and went to a university in Los Angeles. I am tired of the hateful things I hear about Americans in these hostels. The first question I have for all of you who are bashing away at the American people is, "Have you ever been to the USA?"

Silence fell in the room. The angry man who was pointing his finger at me said, "I don't have to go there to know what it's like. I've seen these things on TV."

I replied, "Saying 'no offense' does not excuse you from being offensive. Thinking everybody shares your opinion just shows how small minded you are. Do you really think everything you see on TV is the entire truth about America? Over 300 million people live in my country. Our habits and opinions are as individual as snowflakes. In your travels, I hope you learn not to judge others by their nationality but instead see people as individuals."

To change the subject, someone asked us if the two bikes they saw locked up downstairs were ours, and several others had questions about traveling on a bicycle and how we carried our gear.

This was not the first time anger at America was directed at Cindie and me where international tourists congregated. At first, we thought they were isolated incidents; now we realized a growing trend since the war had started several months earlier.

Later, the guests in the hostel learned Cindie had a nephew in the U.S. Army who was stationed in Iraq. Seeing Cindie cry and turn away from the carnage on TV made them realize the war in Iraq was beyond politics for us.

During our stay in the hostel we got to know individual guests, which helped dispel the stereotype of all Americans being like the ones they saw on TV. The man who believed everyone in the U.S. drove two blocks to McDonald's still refused to speak with us. We did the best we could to ignore him and go about our business.

We were in search of a bicycle shop, as my bicycle's rear wheel had developed a wobble in Bolivia weeks earlier and had been growing steadily worse. I trued it (tightened and loosened spokes to realign the rim) several times, but the annoying wobble would return after a couple of rides.

I had seen wheels behave this way before, and knew

where this rim was heading. Eventually it would start breaking spokes or develop a crack in the rim, and then give out completely.

The biggest bike shop in town was a short walk from where we were staying. Bike riding, for sport and transportation, is popular in Argentina. We had seen cyclists on nice European road bikes (De Rosa, Look, etc.) zipping down the roads in large racing packs, and countless others tooling around on domestic brands.

I was surprised at the size of this bike shop. It was a few weeks before Christmas, and kids were eager to show their parents which bike they wanted on the showroom floor. Posters of cycling legends, including current South American superstars, were in big demand as well. The service department had a long line of people waiting with all manner of bikes and parts in their hands.

Even though the shop employed an army of mechanics, when the sales clerk discovered I was a foreigner the head mechanic was summoned. I wondered if a local would have received such special treatment and felt guilty for this reverse discrimination.

The head mechanic, Jose, was a muscular man with tan marks on his hands from years of wearing bike gloves and covered in grease from pulling apart dirty bikes that morning. Good bike mechanics around the world have the same qualities as Jose; they understand small mechanical things, are true problem solvers, and have a love for the sport and history of cycling. During our introduction, he scanned our bikes and pointed out a frayed brake cable that I had not noticed before.

"I am looking for a strong rim and someone to rebuild my rear wheel," I said as I handed him one of our printed flyers that explains our story and shows pictures of the bikes completely loaded. He read the Spanish side of the paper and asked if he could have it.

I replied, "Yes!"

He pushed my bike into the back of the shop and returned a few minutes later, my rear wheel in his hand. He showed me a crack developing around one of the spokes.

To my surprise, he said, "This shop does not have a high quality rim. I will call around and find one for you." We were sent to a small shop across town, a long walk through Salta's maze of upscale shopping malls and crowded streets.

As we entered the front door of the small bike shop, the owner and sole mechanic greeted us; he had spoken to Jose on the phone and already knew what I needed. He produced a rim from behind the counter and said it was the best one in town; he built my wheel and had it ready for me the next day.

With the new wheel on my bike we were ready to leave Salta and get back to our travels. On the way out of town, the urban area ended abruptly and in its place, cattle grazed on rolling green hills.

We spent the night at a municipal campground near a lake that cost US $0.35 per person. Near our camp, an extended family played football - fathers, sons, uncles and cousins. Manual, a grandfather and the obvious leader of the family,

Our campsite at the municipal campground.

Riding through the arid areas of northern Argentina.

stopped the game and invited me to join them.

I said, "I do not know how to play. I only know how to play American football."

Manual looked at me in shock; I think I was the first man he had ever met who did not play football. I overheard a teenage grandson explain to his grandfather that he had seen American football on TV; he described it as "big guys in helmets running into one another."

Manual grinned and said, "I am sorry, but we only play Argentinean football here." They continued the game. I was surprised at the seriousness of their family game, with rough play that raged on well after dark.

Back on the road the next morning, we climbed slightly and in the blink of an eye, our lush green surroundings changed to brown desert once again. It was as if someone had drawn a line across the earth, with everything above it brown and red and everything below it in different shades of green.

Sheer red walls dominated the landscape; Cindie explained how the interesting shapes of the red sandstone had been sculptured by wind and rain. We rode from formation to formation, stopping every few minutes to take more pictures.

We did not expect conditions to be so dry and were forced to ride longer than we had wanted to in order to locate water. We finally found a small ranch house; I knocked on the door with our 10-liter water bag in hand.

The door opened and a world of creativity revealed itself - ceramics, paintings and woodcarvings. I introduced myself,

Our campsite under a mesquite tree.

Cindie looking for a leak in her tire.

asked for water and a young man led me through the house to the backyard.

This unassuming ranch house was inhabited by an odd combination of artists and goat farmers. Several boys were slaughtering a goat in the shade and never looked up from their work.

I filled our water bag, thanked them and returned to the bikes to find my rear tire had gone flat. We patched it, rode off and found a place to camp under a mesquite tree, towering red rock walls surrounding us. Another day slipped away and I said to Cindie, "The best places to camp are usually free." She agreed.

The next day, we continued down the road through the beautiful canyon. The red rock formations were distinct in shape and had signs at the base of each one with names like the "devil's throat", "the frog", and "the obelisk". It was a bit like a geological theme park. At the end of the day we climbed to a ridge top and saw the wine-growing city of Cafayate sprawled out below.

Cafayate was a friendly city in an arid valley that we liked so much we decided to stay through Christmas. As a present to ourselves, we rented a more expensive room and enjoyed the extra luxuries of a private bathroom, toilet seat, and space to spread out.

Spending Christmas outside the U.S. seemed less hectic; at home we would have been immersed in competitive light shows, tacky decorations, and the overwhelming feeling of being marketed to at every turn. The people in Cafayate, by comparison, made a vacation of this holiday time. Although

Tim and Cindie Travis

Christmas dinner, Argentinian style.

they bought some presents and supplies for family dinners, they mostly relaxed in lawn chairs and drank wine.

A large Argentinean family staying in several rooms at our hotel realized we were far from our families, felt sorry for us, and took us in. Celebrating Christmas day with them felt like the Fourth of July to us; here in the Southern Hemisphere, it was the middle of summer and everyone wore shorts and T-shirts. Our Argentinean style Christmas dinner consisted of several kilos of beef grilled over a large wood fire.

Christmas on the road was difficult for us. We thought about our families; although we did not miss the stress of the holidays, we missed spending time with them. Usually these feelings were suppressed by our busy days of riding and exploring, but spending time with this Argentinean family was a constant reminder of the most important things we gave up

208

Cindie and Tony and the wind sock showing our headwind.

to live our lives down the road.

Tony, the Canadian cyclist we met the day we left Cusco, Peru surprised us with a knock on our door late one evening. He had followed our progress through Bolivia and northern Argentina on our web site and tracked us down in Cafayate. He wanted company for the long desolate stretch ahead; we were happy to have an extra traveling companion. The three of us made plans to leave the next day.

South of Cafayate, Route 40 enters a wild and desolate area. We spent a week crossing wide-open spaces of high desert on a dirt road. One memorable day, the sky behind us had a weird, dark gray look to it and we knew something was wrong. It looked like snow, but it was too warm. We speculated it was locusts and joked about the end of the world.

When the gray mass overtook us, we realized an enormous

Our shelter from the sand storm.

sand storm had caught up with us. Within seconds, I could not see past my front wheel. The sand stung our skin and clogged our lungs. I was afraid of losing track of Cindie in the darkness and confusion, and repeatedly looked back to make sure she was still there. We had no place to go; all we could do was push on, hoping "something" would come along before we were sucked into the heart of the storm. Setting the tent up in the open was impossible, as the wind-whipped sand would have ripped it to shreds.

Just as Cindie began to panic and yell something I could not hear, we rode over a bridge spanning a dry wash. In my early traveling days, well before I met Cindie, I spent a lot of time sleeping under bridges and other free places. If the bridge were big enough to get under, it could provide shelter to survive the storm.

I tried to explain this to Cindie and Tony. They couldn't hear me over the roar of the wind and sand, so I simply pointed at the wash and yelled, "This way!" We quickly pushed our bikes through the wash and under the bridge. We could see and breathe again! We set up the tent and cooked dinner.

Underneath a bridge was a good place in a sand storm, but a bad place when there is the threat of water filling the wash. In the morning, the sand storm turned to rain; we evacuated from the wash and rode on.

A couple days later we rode into Belen, the first sizable town since Cafayate. We badly needed supplies, and a shower to wash the sand from our bodies. It was four o'clock, siesta time; the hotels were closed because everyone was at home asleep. We waited for the hotel manager to wake up and she rented us a room.

New Year's Eve in Argentina was different from what we expected. Argentineans love to party, so we thought there would be an all-out celebration. Cindie and I did not normally go out to bars and discos because it was beyond our budget, but we thought we would treat ourselves to a night on the town. We put on our cleanest clothes and ventured onto the poorly lit streets with Tony.

At 11 p.m., the streets were unexpectedly empty and quiet. We found the doors to a disco were shut, so we walked to a second bar; it was closed as well. We found a man inside sweeping the floor and asked, "When will the New Year's Eve party start?"

He answered, "The bar will open at two a.m."

New Years day and everybody is happy.

I replied, "Isn't it New Year's Eve? It is only 15 minutes to midnight."

Noticing my confusion, he set his broom down and explained, "In Argentina everyone spends New Year's Eve with family, having dinner and toasting the new year at the stroke of midnight. Then the old folks sit around and talk while the kids slip out to the clubs."

We were already tired; staying up for another three hours would be impossible. We went back to our rooms feeling like "the old folks" and went to bed. Cindie and I discussed our mistake of expecting Argentina's cultural traditions to be the same as ours.

We made this same mistake the next morning, thinking everyone would be home sleeping and the roads would be empty. But as we rolled out of town in the early morning light, we heard loud music pumping from downtown. The disco that had been closed the night before was now open - and the party was in full swing. Hundreds of partiers danced, bought drinks and staggered around on the streets. Packed cars with loud music blaring drove from one disco to the other. Drunk drivers were barely able to keep their death traps on the road.

At 11 a.m. we stopped at the only open establishment, a bar, on an otherwise desolate road. We parked the bikes, sat at a table and ordered a large bottle of Sprite; it seems we made another mistake.

In the eyes of the locals, drinking soft drinks on New Year's Day was practically a crime. The celebration was dwindling down from the night before; after nine hours of booze and dancing, the only people left standing were the hardcore drinkers, who crowded around us. Their bad breath and hugging became annoying, but we managed to eat lunch and move on.

We spent the next few days camping and riding our way across the open desert to our next city oasis.

The three of us - Tony, Cindie, and I - took a day off in Chilecito, walked around town and ate ice cream in the plaza.

We were just about ready to head off the next morning when Cindie came running out of the bathroom.

"Tim, Tim! I have blood in my poop!"

I replied, "You know, I have diarrhea but I never looked to see if I had blood as well." We also noticed the blisters inside our mouths.

Our campsite among the cactus.

We delicately asked Tony if he had the same symptoms. All he said was, "I'm not feeling well, either."

Cindie and I debated whether to leave or not because we did not feel too bad, but we were heading off into the desert, a place with no doctors or pharmacies. If we did not deal with our sickness here, we would not be able to once we left. Cindie's travel health book stated if blood was present in the stool, one should see a doctor immediately; we decided to stay. Tony said he felt well enough to ride, so he left about 7:00 a.m. for Villa Union.

Our physician, fresh out of university, checked our blood pressure, temperature, throats and stomach area. She diagnosed us with a bacterial infection in the stomach, and a viral infection in the mouth from drinking contaminated water. We must have come across bad water while camping somewhere along the way from Salta. She prescribed an antibiotic for our stomachs and a cream for the blisters in our mouths. She also was concerned about dehydration, and recommended we rest another day.

From Chilecito, Route 40 turned into a faint dirt road through a desolate area on our map. We climbed for hours up a spectacular canyon to a remote mountain pass. Towards evening we stopped at a house, filled our bags with water and found a place to camp with a sweeping view of the giant cactus and red rock walls that surrounded us.

We had a typical evening when free camping - Cindie pulled together another gourmet dinner of pasta and vegetables from the depths of my bags, and I set up our shortwave radio to catch the evening news on the BBC. After dinner, we turned off the news and watched the stars come out.

The next day we descended into a flat, empty desert and headed for the remote Talampaya National Park. It was hard to believe there was any land in this area worthy of turning into a national park, but it was supposed to be incredibly beautiful - and would be our only water source during the entire day's ride.

At the information center, we learned it was necessary to take a four-wheel drive tour to see the park. The tour was a little expensive, so we agreed to decide in the morning and waited out the afternoon sun in the shade. The day passed slowly; I read a book while Cindie wrote her daily journal on our laptop.

The park emptied three hours before sundown; the only other campers were a couple sitting in lounge chairs, sipping

The geologic phenomena called concretion balls.

Rock formations in Talampaya.

The Information Center for Talampaya National Park.

iced drinks in the shade of their van. We must have looked uncomfortable sitting on the ground in our camp chairs, because when they saw us looking in their direction they waved a bottle of wine in the air and invited us over. We joined them, and Nestor and Maria from Buenos Aires pulled out two more chairs for us.

They spoke Spanish with the distinct accent of the country's capital. Much of our initial conversation was spent sorting out the differences between the Spanish we had learned on the road and the Spanish spoken in Buenos Aires. It was like learning another language all over again.

As the evening slipped away, we drank Argentinean wine and took pictures of a fox and numerous birds. The four of us had a great time and agreed it would be fun to take the 4x4 tour together first thing in the morning.

Chuna, bird of the desert.

Submarine rock.

Instead of putting up the tent, we laid our pads and sleeping bags out on the porch of the information center, put our bikes and gear in Nestor's van for safekeeping and took the first tour of the day into the park.

We saw a lot of wildlife: guanacos (a relative of the llama), mara (like a short-eared rabbit), foxes, wild parrots (very noisy!), and chuna (like a roadrunner). The rock formations were lit up nicely in the morning light.

Nestor offered to take us to the next national park, a few hours away by car and on our route. Riding in the van cut off several days of cycling, but sharing part of Nestor and Maria's vacation was worth it.

They had two large thermoses of hot water for yerba maté; maté for short, the national drink of Argentina. The tea is traditionally drunk through a bombilla, a straw with a filter on the end, from a cup made from a gourd, wood or ornate metal. Maté is called the friendship drink, because many people share the same cup and typically sip it all day long.

We entered Valle de Luna Provincial Park and drove from one rock formation to the next. This park lived up to its name with a surreal, lifeless landscape that looked like the surface of the moon. A guide showed us plant fossils and rock formations with names like "Submarine" and "Mushroom Rock." Of special interest to Cindie were the concretion balls; round rocks formed into the size and shape of a soccer ball through an erosion process.

By the end of the day, Cindie and I were tired; not from cycling or waking up early, but from trying to sort out and absorb everything we had learned at two national parks.

Nester drinking maté.

Reading and translating informative signs and hours of conversations in Spanish took an extra mental effort.

We drove another hour and found a campground, and spent a lot of time with Nestor and Maria over the next two days and nights. Even though they were about the same age as Cindie and I, I was surprised to find they had grown up with the same music. I would have thought they listened to Spanish music instead. I played some tunes from the 70's and 80's I had stored on the computer, and Nester dug around in the van and produced CDs of Electric Light Orchestra and James Taylor. The four of us talked about how growing up with the same music created some common experiences, like remembering what we were doing the day John Lennon was shot.

Our last night with Nestor and Maria was at a noisy

campground next to a big lake in San Juan. It reminded me of spring break in Daytona Beach, Florida - vacationing students drinking and having a good time.

The next morning, we said goodbye to our friends and set off again on our bikes. Riding out of San Juan was confusing, but we eventually found some friendly cyclists who happily helped us with directions.

The ride to Mendoza was flat with a strong headwind. After a night in a truck drivers' hotel, we completed the final 112 kilometers (69 miles) and arrived in downtown Mendoza.

Cindie and I enjoyed Mendoza, a beautiful city with tree-lined streets, outdoor cafes and elegantly dressed people shopping in upscale stores and malls. All the glitz and fashion made it noticeably more expensive compared to Argentinean cities in the north.

Mendoza had a type of restaurant we had not seen before in Latin America, called the Tenedor Libre (free fork), an all-you-can eat-buffet that included steak grilled on a wood fire. We gorged ourselves there several times during our one-week stay.

We left Mendoza on a high-speed four-lane highway accompanied by the deafening roar of the traffic flying by.

Cindie yelled over the noise, "My bike is not shifting right." She pointed to the side of the road and we pulled over.

I examined her drive train and said, "You have a bent link on your chain. I've seen you wear out tires and brake pads before, but never a chain."

Her reaction made me laugh; instead of being upset, she

Tim riding toward one of the many tunnels between Mendoza, Argentina and Los Andes, Chile.

Tim at Aconcagua National Park.

beamed with pride. "Does this mean I'm getting stronger?"

I replied, "Well, yes, most likely."

She acted as if it was a major accomplishment. I, on the other hand, was not so happy; I had to fix the chain.

Cindie asked to keep the bad links I had removed. My guess is, she still has these twisted sections of worthless chain somewhere. I can't wait to see her excitement when she breaks her first spoke!

The Andes mountain chain generally defines the border between Argentina and Chile, our next destination; to leave, we had to ride uphill for four days. Toward the top, the road became steep and we encountered a headwind so strong we traveled only 16 kilometers (10 miles) in three hours. During this grind, a gust of wind hit us hard and knocked Cindie off her bike. I prepared to deliver a speech about how we had no choice but to push on; before I could say it she stood up, dusted herself off and got back on the bike.

Our plan was to camp for the night in Aconcagua National Park, but we were exhausted and wanted to be indoors away from the wind. Two kilometers (1.2 miles) before the turn-off to the park, we found a hostel that caters to groups climbing Aconcagua, the highest mountain peak outside of Asia.

In the hostel, we heard the familiar sound of people speaking English with a North American accent. We introduced ourselves to members of the group and learned they were a mountain climbing club from Boulder, Colorado. At dinner, we listened intently to the stories from their three-week adventure ascending the challenging peak.

The next day we said goodbye to the group as they boarded a bus for Santiago to fly home. We kept in contact with one member, Roger Wendell, who later interviewed us on his radio talk show several months later. The MP3 file of that interview is located in our media section of our web site (www.downtheroad.org).

It was a few kilometers straight up a rough dirt road to Aconcagua National Park. The park has a small ranger station and a busy shack that collects fees from climbers and trekkers totaling hundreds of US dollars each. We went on a short hike and took pictures of the beautiful peak before returning to our bicycles and continuing to the border.

People often ask us, "What are the scariest moments of your travels?"

I always answer that other than the day we left home, my narrow escapes from thieves are the scariest for me; Cindie tells her stories of riding through unlit tunnels, and always at the top of her list is the one we were about to enter. Below was what she wrote about our ride.

"I do not like riding through long, narrow, black tunnels. When we came to tunnel number 14, near the border of Argentina and Chile, it was the worst-case scenario: Uphill, into the wind and pitch black.

We tried to hitch a ride through, but no one would stop to pick us up this close to the border. The only thing we could do was wait until traffic cleared. When we had our chance, Tim urged me on by yelling, "Go, Cindie, go!"

I pedaled as fast as I could into the dark abyss, and the

tunnel went from barely lit to pitch black. I couldn't see a thing. I was frightened out of my mind. As I rode deeper into the tunnel, my head was swimming I felt disoriented. I feared I would hit an unseen hole in the pavement and fall off my bike.

A car entered the tunnel from the other direction and illuminated it. I discovered I was in the middle of the road and had to move over to let the car pass. I raced to the end of the tunnel and burst into the sunlight, lungs burning and adrenaline pumping to the point I was shaking. Tim was right behind me. Not seconds after we emerged from the tunnel, a truck with a load of new cars rushed by; I was glad we had not met him a few moments earlier."

I waited until Cindie had calmed down enough to ride the remaining two kilometers to the final tunnel, which was closed to cyclists. We waited for a border guard to call a truck and take us through, free of charge. This tunnel was well lit; Cindie suggested to the driver that trucks pick up cyclists before tunnel number 14. On the other side, we were out of Argentina and knocking on the door to Chile.

A building in Salta with a mural of Che.

Riding through yet another tunnel.

Chapter 9
Chile: Finding the Endless Road

Tim crossing into Chile.

The Chilean immigration official leafed through the pages of my passport, reviewing all the stamps.

"How many countries have you ridden through to reach Chile?"

"Ten, not including the USA."

He held up his index finger and proudly said, "But Chile will always be number one."

Chileans are fiercely proud of the beauty and prosperity of their country. The beauty could be seen from the immigration office window; jagged peaks towered above alpine valleys dotted with yellow and purple wildflowers swaying in the summer breeze.

The prosperity was felt when Cindie exchanged money. Chile was experiencing rapid trade growth with North America, strengthening the Chilean peso against the United States dollar. The exchange rate was 560 pesos to the dollar; a year earlier, it had been 1500 pesos to the dollar. The cost of traveling in Chile had tripled for us in one year's time.

We left the border zone and rode into Portillo, a famous ski area with rocky slopes bathed in the summer sun. We coasted a few meters to a hostel that catered to winter snow sport tourists; now, it was empty except for the family who lived there.

Posters of skiers having fun on the slopes covered the walls and brought back memories of the wonderful adrenaline rush of speeding down ski runs. I missed my days of working at ski resorts and living the life of a ski bum; in our travels around the world, we try to avoid cold weather and snow.

We stayed in Portillo longer than we originally had planned. I did not know it then, but I was in the beginning stages of burnout. We had been traveling hard for months. The packing and unpacking everyday was starting to get to me. I wasn't homesick; but I was tired of being uprooted everyday and craved sitting indoors and being domestic. Things that hadn't bothered me before - not knowing where we were going to sleep every night, always being the strangers in town - now were irritating me.

Cindie reacted differently to life on the road; she had energy and seemed to be as fresh as the day we had left. In Portillo, I thought I needed only a week off to get back in the

The switchbacks near Portillo.

groove. Time would reveal just how strung out I was.

From Portillo, the ride to the city of Los Andes was one long coast back to sea level. We stopped to cool our brakes at the edge of a guardrail and looked down at the tight switchbacks looping their way to lower altitude.

We took our time through countless 180-degree turns. The thin mountain air brought the scenery alive, but we had to watch the road; one mistake meant falling over the side to certain death.

On the way down, we met a Swiss man running around the world; his girlfriend followed him on a motorcycle. I wished we had had more time to talk, but he was going to have a long day in front of him running up the hill we had just descended.

We rode into Los Andes late and checked into a hotel.

The Swiss runner and his girlfriend.

Cindie and I talked into the night about our options for heading south. In my tired state, nothing sounded appealing. The main obstacle for Cindie was Chile's capital city of Santiago, as she did not like to ride in dense urban traffic. We decided to skip the traffic and bus ahead to the Lake District of southern Chile, an area known among cyclists for its distinct beauty and quiet roads.

We took a bus through Santiago to Temuco, the starting point of our tour through the Lake District. We found a room in a back alley hostel, and stayed an extra day to finish some work at one of the town's many Internet cafes.

When we left Arizona almost two years earlier, we rode toward the equator. From Ecuador we slowly rode south away from it, but never enough to feel like we were at latitude. This was the first time on our trip we were more than 35 degrees away from the equator, and we noticed the cooler climate at our new southern latitude. Here we rode past numerous dairy farms and hardwood trees. The midday sun was noticeably lower on the horizon - but in the northern sky, not the southern like in Arizona.

We found a campground next to a creek of beautiful clean water. We set up the tent and Cindie made dinner on our camp stove. It was so peaceful; I never turned on our short-wave radio to listen to the news, content instead to watch the sun reflect off the flowing water. For me, anything felt better than riding my bike.

Another cyclist rode into the campground and we invited her to camp with us. Suzanne from Munich, Germany was traveling alone, the first female solo bike tourist we had met. It was comforting to be in a country where women felt safe to explore alone on a bike. We discovered we were heading in the same direction and decided to ride together for a few days.

Usually I could keep up with Cindie, even with my enormous load of gear and an extra week's worth of food; but my cycling performance had decreased. As I watched Cindie and Suzanne pull farther and farther ahead absorbed in conversation, I recognized I had felt this way before.

In my teens and twenties, I raced road bikes. Every fall, late in the season, burnout would hit my competitors and me and we struggled even on the easiest of rides. We knew it was time for the season to end and took an extended break off the bikes over the winter. I realized that after two years of travel, I needed several weeks away from cycling.

231

Volcano Llaima looms ahead.

Tim and Susanna taking a break.

Chile: Finding the Endless Road

Because Cindie and I lived nomadically and followed the seasons, my body had been thinking it was summer for almost two years. The Chilean climate, with its long days, green trees and blooming flowers, told my brain it was summer and time to ride; but my legs remembered all the months of cycling and wanted a break.

Even though Cindie was riding better than ever she was not used to waiting for me. She rode on with Suzanne for over 30 minutes before wondering where I was. They had to wait a long time for me to catch up and when I arrived, I could see the look of concern on Cindie's face; she knew something was wrong with me.

As we rode into Conguillio National Park, our road turned to smooth dirt and a huge, permanently snow-capped volcano dominated the scenery. We took a rest day at the park campground and I worked on writing a long newsletter. The only place to plug in my computer was near the shared bathroom. At first I was alone but before long, I was entertaining a group of people with a slideshow of our travels from Mexico to Chile.

The next day we rode through a lifeless volcanic landscape on a road made of black cinders and ash that climbed over lava flows and then descended into a flat valley, leaving the volcanic landscape behind. We stayed the night in Cunco.

On our way out of town the next day, we rode through a construction zone with bulldozers and graders. It was difficult to keep my heavily loaded bike upright in the deep, loose gravel. The noise of the machines echoed in my ears and diesel exhaust poisoned my lungs.

Tim and Cindie Travis

Volcano Llaima in Conguillio National Park.

Riding over a lava flow.

Suddenly, something happened to my bike. I lost power. I turned the pedals; the cassette (rear cogs) rotated, but it was no longer engaged with the hub so I was no longer moving forward. I had to get off my bike and push it to the side so a dump truck could get by. It took some time for Cindie to figure out that I had a mechanical problem and ride back. Suzanne never stopped to wait, probably thinking one of us had only a flat tire.

We walked back to Cunco and the small bike shop I had noticed earlier, but the shop only had parts for kids' bikes. The owner suggested we ride the bus to Temuco and visit one of the high-end shops in the city. We checked back into our same room, thinking it was for only one more night.

The next day we rode the bus into Temuco and used the Internet to make a VOIP phone call to the hub manufacture. When I described my problem, they said it was not the hub that broke but the free hub attached to it. Apparently, I had neglected to do the proper maintenance on the free hub for two years and it eventually broke. Upon my promise to regularly clean and lube the next one, they said they would send me a new hub.

We found a modern bike shop that caters to the local mountain and road-racing scenes. The owner was helpful, even though I had trouble understanding his thick Chilean accent. We arranged to have the new hub sent to his shop and have his best mechanic build a wheel with a new rim and spokes. The owner called the post office and was informed it would take a week for the hub to clear customs. We went back to Cunco with unexpected time on our hands.

Cindie updating her journal.

We took long walks and met people in the small community. At night, we listened to music while we cleaned and repaired our neglected gear. The tent bag was falling apart and needed duct tape; the hole in the shower bag needed to be sewn; the outside pocket of Cindie's pannier had come apart at the seam and needed to be glued. The zippers on our tent were failing - we could use one door, but the other door was permanently closed because the zipper was broken. We called it "the forbidden door."

We also used the time to discuss what it would take to produce a book about our travels. Every time I emailed a newsletter to our subscription list, people encouraged me to write more; a book seemed to be a natural progression.

We had been carrying two reference books about the

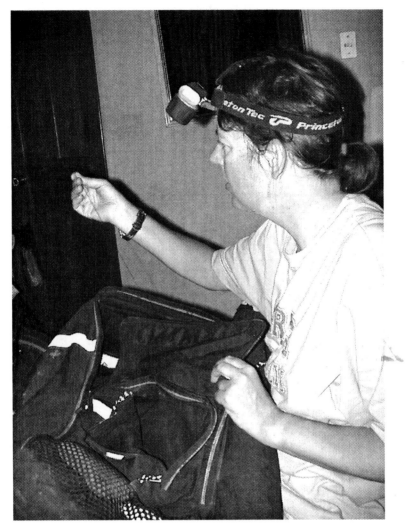

Cindie fixing Tim's pannier.

publishing business. One described how to submit manu-
scripts to publishers and typical contracts for first time au-
thors, while the other described how to write and self-publish
your own book. After reading both approaches, Cindie and I
concluded we were too independent-minded to have a publisher take control of our book. We easily decided that if we

237

were to go through with this, we would self-publish.

We researched further and discussed options for self-publishing our own book. Cunco had a slow but cheap Internet cafe, and we found the current costs for having an artist create a cover design, professional editing, printing and storing books. We typed an outline that summarized tasks with timelines and costs. Our biggest concern about self-publishing was the upfront cost; it would be a substantial amount of our remaining travel funds.

We also knew writing a book while we were on the go was impossible. Traveling to new places kept us busy on the computer, adding photos and writing daily journals for our web site. We estimated it would take three months of staying in one place to write the book. We had not yet taken a rest stop for that length of time, but it was appealing to me to have a long break from the bikes; this could be my off-season.

Cindie asked, "Where is the perfect place to stop? It would have to be affordable enough to get a room, have daily Internet access, and places to hike."

All I could say was, "I don't know, but we'll recognize paradise when we stumble into it." I just hoped I would have the energy to get there.

The hub cleared customs, my rear wheel was built, and we returned to the road after a week's stay in Cunco. With the idea of creating a book on my mind, I lost interest in my regular newsletter and the web site.

Cindie describes our remaining travels through Chile and on to Bariloche, Argentina.

Dirt road to the campground near the river Tolten.

When we left Cunco, it was refreshing to get my legs moving again. Tim and I had drifted in opposite directions; I was energetic and could pedal for hours, while he struggled and looked tired. I wanted to take advantage of the long summer days and increase our time in the saddle; he wanted to cut our days in half, lie around camp and talk about creating a book. Every day on the road, we repeated this tug of war. It was the first time we were not in rhythm together and it felt strange.

We rode to a campground and set up our tent by the river Tolten, where people fishing for trout and salmon floated by in small wooden boats. While making dinner, we met Victor and his family from Santiago; he was a scoutmaster and specialized in astronomy. He showed us many constellations in the sparkling evening sky, including the Southern Cross. Because I could not see the Big Dipper (seen only in the Northern Hemisphere), I felt a bit disoriented and

Scout patches given to Tim.

Tim fishing on the Tolten river.

a long way from home.

Our discussion turned to the Boy Scouts and Robert Baden-Powell, who founded the Scouts in England around 1908. The organization was present in many countries, and in Chile they combined the Boy and Girl Scouts. When Victor discovered Tim had spent several years as a Scout in the U.S., he carefully cut the Chilean Scout patch off his shirt and gave it to Tim, who gratefully accepted it by exchanging a funny handshake.

While at the campsite I collected drinking water from a tap that I had assumed was potable, like all the other water taps in Chile. Out of curiosity, I followed the pipe to a pump house with an electric pump and was horrified to see the intake pipe went down a slope and into the river.

Oh, no!

I suddenly realized the water we had been drinking for the last 24 hours came directly from the river. I feared disaster would strike and it was only a matter of time before we were both sick.

The next day we rode to Villarica, a resort town with beautiful views of a snow capped volcano and the surrounding lake. We had lunch at an outdoor cafe and ordered hot dogs, which arrived on hand-carved wooden holders. Tim mentioned to the waiter he had never seen a special holder for a hot dog and as we were leaving, the waiter returned with a brown paper bag and gave it to Tim.

Later, when we looked inside, we found two hot dog holders neatly wrapped in napkins. Tim commented with a grin, "My favorite souvenirs are the gifts people have given us along the way."

We rode out of Villarica and camped at Pucura for the night. Tim was not feeling well; he had a touch of diarrhea, did not eat dinner,

The beach at Pucura.

Not much room on the road for a truck and a cyclist.

and when he went to bed he had a slight fever. I was not surprised and felt guilty for being careless about our drinking water.

While lying in our tent, Tim complained of nausea. Before I knew it he forced open the forbidden door and vomited outside the tent. I was relieved he had made it outside in time; it would have been a nightmare if he hadn't. The sound of him vomiting was stomach wrenching and brought tears to my eyes. Then the smell hit me and almost made me sick, too.

He was white as a ghost and barely had the energy to go to the bathroom and clean up. While Tim was in the bathroom, I tried to fix the broken tent door. Mosquitoes zoomed around in the tent, buzzing around my ears - the most irritating sound I know.

It was after midnight, the mosquitoes were having a picnic and the smell of sickness was in the air; not one of our better nights. The river water we drank two days ago had been contaminated, and Tim got the worst of it.

In the morning, Tim was so weak. I rode into town in search of antibiotics. My first stop was the pharmacy; the pharmacist tried to sell me things I did not want to buy, like Imodium to stop the diarrhea. I declined his suggestions and asked for an antibiotic; he replied, "Not without a prescription."

We were back in a country where I needed a prescription to buy an antibiotic.

I wandered around town and found a 24-hour urgent care clinic where the doctor spoke fluent English. I explained to him we were traveling on bicycles and Tim was so sick he could not ride into town. We discussed Tim's symptoms, and he gave me a sample packet with a course of ciprofloxacin, an antibiotic for bacteria infections.

Camping in our leaky tent.

Thermal hot springs at Marquecura.

Elated, I jumped back on my bike and pedaled as fast as I could to camp and gave Tim the antibiotics. For some reason, I never became ill from drinking contaminated water; only Tim ended up paying for my mistake. I felt awful.

Tim was still worn out, but we had had a good night's sleep and a short day of riding over a mountain pass called Cuesta Los Aniques. Unfortunately, the weather quickly turned from sunny and warm to cloudy and cold and we stopped at the pass to catch our breath.

Finding a place to pitch the tent was not so easy; the privately owned land around us was fenced. To the sound of rolling thunder, we rode down the hill and found a place to camp near a bridge; a steady rain continued the entire night.

Our leaky tent dripped here and there. I wiggled my body around the wet spots, but still had a drip over my head. I used our dry bag to shield myself from getting wet; the constant dripping sound drove me crazy and made me restless.

Tim was not sleeping either; how could he, with me accidentally kicking him whenever I moved? The tent was on its last legs and every time it rained, I felt like I was bailing water out of a boat rather than having protection from the elements.

The next day it continued to rain; a little at first, and then a deluge. We took cover in a bus stop, waited out the rain, and then rode to a hot springs resort called Thermals Marquecura. I dreamed of sitting in a hot spring and convinced Tim to ride the extra eight kilometers (five miles) past our turn. Tim is always willing to explore a new place, especially when I have my heart set on it, and did not mind going out of our way.

The last two kilometers (1.2 miles) to the hot spring were up

Riding onto the ferry.

Cindie picking berries on the side of the road.

a steep muddy road. While Tim rode the entire way, I could not. When we finally arrived at the resort, we were soaked to the skin and elected to get a cabin instead of camping in our leaky tent.

At the hot springs, I was like a kid in a candy store. I found a concrete hot spring pool, a tinta (wooden bathtub) with very hot mineralized water, a shower room with hot and cold water and a mud spring full of kids covered in mud from head to toe.

We stayed an extra day at the thermal hot springs; our gear was still too wet to go on. Tim stayed in the cabin while I spent the day hopping from the hot spring, to the mud spring, to the shower and back again to the hot spring. When I returned to our cabin with pruned skin after hours of soaking in hot water, Tim showed me a detailed outline for the first chapter of our book on the computer. The sparkle in his eye told me the gears in his mind were turning. Deep down, I knew this would change my life someday - and someday soon.

With dry gear and relaxed bodies, we rode back to the intersection and on toward Puerto Fuy. The terrain was constantly up and down; the road was gravel and in some areas, the gravel and rocks were too large for me to plow through. The constant battle to keep my bike upright wore me out.

The scenery, on the other hand, was breathtaking - glacial lakes, volcanoes, and the road was lined with my favorite fruit, blackberries. It was berry season and every time we took a break, I ate so many my fingertips were purple and my wrists had scratches from the thorny vines.

We arrived in Puerto Fuy just in time to catch the ferry. While on board, the porter asked if we could translate something from

English to Spanish. The ship was new and the crew couldn't understand the manual on how to maintain its septic system. All that time I spent reviewing septic system plans for the State of Arizona was now paying off!

My Spanish was not good enough to translate a technical document word for word, but I explained the concept. The crew gave us free passage in exchange for my help.

We arrived in Puerto Pirihueico and spent our last night in Chile camping on the bank of the lake.

We thought we could make it to San Martin, Argentina the next day, but the border crossing and custom checks slowed us down. We camped off the road near a spring, and in the morning awoke to the sound of a herd of horses running past our tent. Tim jumped out and waved them around us; this was impressive, as he had not even had his coffee yet.

We crossed the Andes again; this was an easier crossing than before. The mountains were lower in this part of the continent. Now we were in San Martin, Argentina, a quiet resort town on a lake. Argentina was less expensive than Chile, and I was happy not to see our money flying out of our wallet so quickly. We stayed at the campground in the north end of town, where fellow bike tourists and locals alike seemed to congregate.

On the way to Villa la Angostura the pavement ended and the dirt began. We passed a beautiful lake; it was so clear and calm we could see the surrounding mountains in its reflection. The dirt road climbed and dropped steadily through this stunning area, but the traffic was extremely heavy. It was summer break; the local tourists were out in their cars and students were standing on the side of the road hitching rides. We were frustrated with (and a little bit angry

248

at) the drivers that sprayed gravel on us as they flew by. They were in a rush and did not slow down, even on the steeper sections of the road.

We were tired by the time we reached Villa la Angostura, so we stopped at the first campground we saw and I bought a few steaks from the supermarket for dinner. The campground host wanted to charge us for the use of chairs at our campsite and I was more than irritated. I began to think maybe I needed a break from the road, as well.

In the morning it took two hours to pack up. I felt like the Energizer bunny running out of battery life; maybe Tim was right about needing a break.

Our next stop was Bariloche, Argentina.

Tim and Cindie Travis

Lake near Portillo, Chile.

Cindie crossing the border from Chile to Argentina.

Chapter 10
Patagonia: Taking the Big Leap

Tim near Villa la Angostura.

The moment we rode into Bariloche, I knew it was a place worth getting to know. Downtown had an incredible view of a large, pristine glacial lake in one direction and green, forested mountains in the other. When we discovered the city bus could drop us off at dozens of places for day hikes, Cindie and I agreed Bariloche was perfect for taking a break from the bikes and working on a book. The problem was we still wanted to take advantage of the late summer weather and see some of the far south before winter arrived. It was obvious there was not enough time to ride the famous Carreteras Austral south to Tierra De Fuego and also go on several multi-day hikes in the famous National Parks to the far south. We had

Downtown Bariloche.

St. Bernard puppies.

to choose between the two adventures.

In our youth hostel we met an Australian named Justin, who had camping and hiking gear and wanted to go trekking (backpacking) as well. Cindie, Justin, and I agreed to rent a car and go on a three-week trekking and sightseeing trip, and then return to Bariloche. We bought backpacks for the multi-day hikes and a pair of light hiking boots to replace my worn tennis shoes, stored our bikes at the hostel for a small fee and excitedly took off on our new trekking adventure.

Although we went to some of the best trekking locations in the world - Torres Del Paine in Chile and Fritz Roy in Argentina - my mind was on creating a book. When we were not walking I was writing down my thoughts about chapter titles and cover designs on any spare paper I could find. It was frustrating not to be able to do more than make outlines and sketches. It felt like a lost month.

The intensity with which I focused on the book reminded me of the years before we left Arizona, when I was research-ing and planning our trip. Back then, the thought of leaving it all behind consumed me. I did not know where the trip would lead us, but I knew we had to go. Now, I felt compelled to express myself by writing our story in a book, even though I had never aspired to be an author before. Once again, I did not know where this new road would lead me.

Physically, I was still burned out from the previous months of riding. On the hikes, I fell behind and Cindie and Justin had to wait. I could not explain why; I felt tired and just wanted to sit and make notes about the book.

The highlight of our trek was the Perito Moreno Glacier,

Perito Moreno Glacier.

Viewing platform for Perito Moreno Glacier.

where we were extremely lucky to witness a phenomenon that had not occurred for 16 years.

Perito Moreno Glacier flows into two lakes; Argentino and Escondido. The two lakes meet at the glacier and are separated by a small peninsula. Every so often, the glacier grows far enough to reach the peninsula and form a dam between the two lakes. Once the dam forms, Lake Escondido rises about ten meters (30 feet) higher than Lake Argentino. The water pressure on the glacier gradually forms a tunnel through the ice dam that grows to a violent flow, thus equalizing the level of the lakes.

As water flowed through the tunnel it sped up the melting process and to our delight, house-sized chunks of ice fell from the glacier into the swift river accompanied by the tremendous sounds of cracks, booms and splashes. We watched for hours each day and saw the tunnel enlarge. I set up our tripod and videotaped scenes of the mountains of ice cleaving off the tunnel and collapsing into the water. We spent two days watching the glacier along with some 3,000 other people. This was such a special phenomenon; it was shown live on TV throughout Argentina and was regularly featured in the international press.

I returned to Bariloche from our three-week trip with sore feet, a few pictures, and several pages of notes about our book written on the backs of used maps and park brochures. First I had to update the web site; I had not worked on it since Cunco, Chile and our first serious discussion about the book. We had weeks of pictures to sort out, label and place on the web site.

Glacier before rupture.

Glacier after rupture.

Patagonia: Taking the Big Leap

When we finally downloaded our email, we realized our lengthy break from the web site had resulted in people, concerned for our well being, frantically writing to us and asking for our whereabouts. After answering these emails and tying up the South American section of the site, I was finally free to work on the project that everything inside me screamed for: The book.

We stayed in Bariloche for almost three months and spent most days rewriting newsletters and working on edits. We took long walks along the lakeshore and mountain trails, discussing our progress and developing ideas. It was a very exciting and creative time for us.

I found it particularly challenging to fine tune the introductory chapter describing where the idea of traveling for years came from and how I talked Cindie into letting go of her old life. It was difficult to describe the process by which a couple with professional careers living in a comfortable home stuffed with possessions became a pair of nomads, carrying everything we owned on two bicycles and sleeping in a tent. Typing all this out really made us revisit what we had done with our lives. At the time, we were so determined to leave it never occurred to us that our decision was so big and unique.

Writing the final chapter was an exercise in describing what we had learned during the first year of our journey, and what we believed were the deeper meanings of our travels. I had thought about this for months during the countless, silent hours on my bike, but never dreamed I would have to take such abstract, life-changing concepts and put them into

Granite peaks in Torres Del Paine National Park.

words. When it was all painstakingly written out and edited several times, I was proud of what I had accomplished.

During our three months in Bariloche, we witnessed early fall turn into winter, the bright red and orange leaves contrasting with the white snow line that slowly descended the mountains. Seeing the seasons change was something we had not experienced in a long time, and it was comforting to our internal clocks.

If only for a few months, we lived like everyone else. We did not need a tourist map to find things in the area, and we made several friends around town. The time off the bike was just what I needed. By June 2004, I was ready to leave early winter behind and fly to an early summer back in Indiana. I was itching to do some riding there on our tandem (the one we got married on). My cycling burnout was over.

Patagonia: Taking the Big Leap

When we felt the book was done and as polished as we could make it ourselves, we hired a professional editor to double check the spelling and grammar. This would require a few weeks' turnaround, so we booked a flight to the U.S. to visit our families before heading to the next continent and continuing our trip.

It was cheaper to take an overnight bus to Buenos Aires and then take a flight to the U.S., so we prepared our bikes to fly. A local bike shop boxed them, and we paid a shop employee to drive us back to the hostel with our two large boxes.

On the bus, we knew our South America trip was over and we let ourselves think about our two years of travel. We were surprised at how long we stuck to our original plan; we had indeed "followed the spine of the Andes Mountains south all the way to Southern Chile."

We had our tickets to Indiana, but had not booked tickets beyond that. Our original plan was to go to Africa next, but we knew we had the freedom to go anywhere we wanted.

Cindie was tired of the developing world and wanted to go to Europe next. In Europe she would have all comforts of home - stocked supermarkets, clean water and functioning toilets. But Europe was an expensive place to travel, and our budget would limit our activities.

I wanted to stick to the original plan and go to Africa; it sounded so exciting and exotic. But undeniably, Africa would be some hard traveling; I felt if we went to such a difficult place now, Cindie would want to quit the trip and stay in the U.S. At this point I knew it would be tricky to talk her into the more challenging places in the world.

Crossing a raging river in Torres de Paine.

A third option was to go to Southeast Asia and China, where we could afford hotels most nights and dinners out. It sounded easier than Africa, and less expensive than Europe. But the final decision could wait a few weeks until we started shopping for flights.

This brought us back to the big decision about going ahead

with the book. To me, writing and editing took only an investment of time and was a good excuse to hang out in Bariloche; hiring a cover artist, finding an order fulfillment company and printing thousands of books would be expensive. I was uncharacteristically cautious, while Cindie was surprisingly eager.

I asked her, "Do you really think this project will work? There is still so much we do not know about putting together a book. I bet there is some roadblock we haven't discovered yet. We could blow a lot of savings that we'll never see again."

Cindie thought for a moment. "I'm aware of the risk. Ending our trip early is unthinkable, but if it works we could travel longer than we originally planned...possibly much, much longer."

"Do you realize if we gamble and lose, we will have to go home early and get jobs? After all this freedom, I'm not sure I could go back to the work week grind. Besides, I'm not ready to quit the road. If we go home early, what continents do you want to skip?"

"But Tim, if the book works out we could travel longer. Think of it this way; what places do you want to add?"

"You know me, I'm a dreamer. I have always wanted to visit India, Russia, Japan, and more; but I never mentioned them because we didn't have the time or money. I can go on and on. Don't get me started thinking about all the places I want to go. I could daydream for weeks."

"Then don't just dream, Tim; make it a reality. I remember before we started on this crazy adventure, I was afraid

Tim trekking in Torres de Paine.

of leaving my career and comfortable life to live on a bicycle. You said so many things that convinced me to take a chance and go - like, 'The biggest killer of dreams is fear.' But the thing you said that really made me want to risk it all was, 'It's like taking a giant leap in the dark and believing we will land in a safe place.' In other words, we just need to believe in ourselves and our ability to adjust to whatever happens, and trust that everything will work out.

"Back then, you were right to talk me into this nomadic life on the road - and look how far we have come! Overcoming all the roadblocks and putting this book together is no different from all the other obstacles in our path that we've conquered, like crossing huge mountains or enduring torrential rainstorms. We can self-publish this book and travel beyond our wildest dreams. Don't hold back. Think of all the places we could go if time was not a limitation. Think out of the box and what our travels could be without an end. True freedom! Not just freedom for a limited amount of time, but true and real freedom!"

"But Cindie, we've met many travelers who've tried different things to stay on the road or at least extend their trip in creative ways, but they never seemed to work. Up to now, I've only thought of traveling for a limited amount of time. The idea our travels could somehow be a permanent lifestyle is a whole new way of looking at things. It really is mind blowing. What a beautifully strange career choice." The addictive nature of freedom was tempting me to risk it all.

"Tim, I know people have told you not to risk our investment because we will fail. There will always be naysayers. Doesn't this remind you of those years before we left? You were talking about going on this big bike trip, and everyone told you it was a pipe dream. You ignored them then, and you'll just have to do it again. I'm ready to choose my own destiny, make another dream come true, and commit to seeing this through.

"Come on, I have never known you to let fear stand in your way; take another leap in the dark with me. There are no guarantees where we'll land, but at least we will land there together."

I looked down at the floor of the bus and said, "I don't know."

"Tim, Look out the window and tell me what you see."

"I see the road we are on, but I already know where it goes. I also see a less traveled road disappearing into the horizon. But I have no way of knowing where it would take us; I can't see past the horizon."

"Tim, if there is one thing you have taught me on this trip, it's that you can't see past the horizon with your eyes; you have to use courage and imagination. Do not be afraid to see past the horizon."

"You're right. With my imagination, I can see tomorrow. Let's do it. Let's jump together!

As the road beyond the horizon came into focus, Cindie put her head on my shoulder and squeezed my hand tightly. At that moment we took our second giant leap in the dark and "*The Road That Has No End*" was found.

Appendix A
Equipment List

Fully loaded touring bike.

This equipment list contains the gear we used in South America and beyond. We shared items whenever possible.

Bicycles - Two touring bikes: each with 26-inch wheels, front and rear racks, bike computers, water bottles, cages, tail lights, kickstands, touring specific saddles, and clipless pedals.

Panniers (bike saddlebags) front and rear waterproof panniers, seat bags, handlebar bags, and repair kit. We used adjustable bungee cords to hold the tent, sleeping bags, and pads on top of our rear racks. After South America, we added a clip on shoulder strap attachment to convert a pannier into daypack for off bike hikes and shopping.

The tent we used in South America.

Our gasoline burning stove.

Camping for Two.

- tent and repair kit
- tent stakes
- ground cloth
- light weight tarp (used to cover the bikes)
- sleeping bags and water-proof dry bag stuff sacks
- sleeping pads with camp chair attachment

Water Purification and Storage

- 10-liter (2.6 gallon) water storage bag/solar shower
-3 bicycle water bottles (each)
- 0.2 micron ceramic water filter and repair kit
- iodine tablets

Stove

- gasoline burning camp stove
- wind screen
- lighter
- cleaning and repair kit
- fuel bottle (size varies)

Kitchen Utensils

- cooking knife
- small flexible cutting board
- can opener (army style)
- spices – salt, pepper, garlic, cinnamon, ginger, and more
- olive oil
- resealable bags
- dish drying cloth

Food Staples

- coffee
- sweetener
- powdered milk
- peanut butter
- bread or tortillas
- oatmeal
- pasta and sauce
- rice
- fresh, canned, or dried vegetables
- instant noodles
- canned meat
- powdered soup

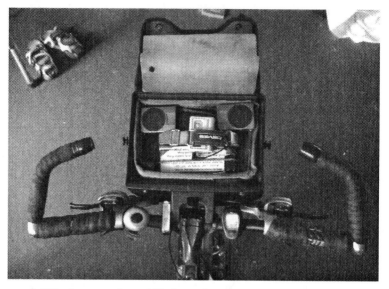

MP3 player and amplified speakers in Tim's handlebar bag.

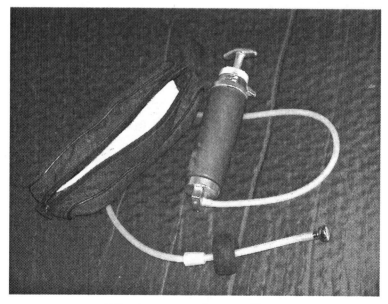

0.2 micron ceramic water filter.

Electronics

- laptop computer and power cord
- microphone
- network cable
- MP3 player
- external amplified speakers
- headphones
- shortwave radio

Camera

-video/still camera
- extra high capacity battery
- connector cables
- power cord for charging
- lense cleaning kit
- zoom, wide angle, polar-ized, and UV lenses
- mini-tripod
- blank mini DV tapes
- extra flash memory

Power and Electricity

- AA rechargeable batteries (several)
- AA battery charger and cord
- extension cord with three way splitter (US plugs)
- international plug adaptors
- light socket adaptor (T)

Other Electronics

- flash light/headlamps
- altimeter/compass watch

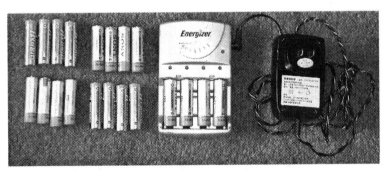

Battery charger and AA rechargeable batteries.

Our pots and pans.

We used a T Adaptor to convert a light socket into an electrical outlet.

First Aid Kit

- international health and first aid manual
- adhesive bandages (various sizes)
- elastic-wrap bandage
- gauge, pads and roll
- antiseptic wipe
- safety pins
- medical tape
- folding scissors
- tweezers
- antibacterial cream
- burn/first aid cream
- antifungal cream
- eye drop antibiotic
- aspirin/ibuprofen
- antihistamine
- Moleskin
- antacid tablets

Antibiotics

- Doxycycline (Malaria)
- Metronidazole (for Amoebiasis and Giardiasis)
- Ciprofloxacin (for bacillary dysentery, shigellosis)
- Amoxycillin (for broad spectrum for general use such as infected cuts)
- Mebendazole (for worms)
- Thermometer

Health

- lip balm
- sunscreen
- insect repellent and mosquito coils
- multivitamins
- earplugs
- eye mask (blindfold for sleeping)

Toiletries

- toilet paper
- toothbrush and toothpaste
- quick drying towel
- brush/comb
- shampoo and conditioner
- bar soap
- razor
- fingernail clippers
- small mirror
- wet wipes

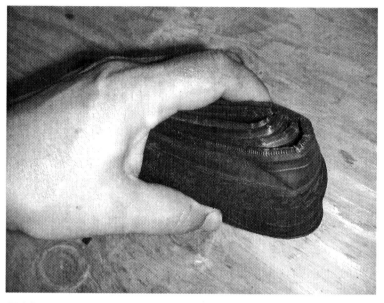

Folding spare tires are small and can be a life saver in remote areas.

Cindie viewing wildlife with her mini-binoculars.

Cycling Clothing (per person)

- 2 cycling shorts
- 1 – 2 short sleeve jerseys
- 1 wool long sleeve jersey
- 1 cycling tights
- 1 pair cycling gloves
- helmet
- sunglasses
- bandana

Off Bike Clothing (per person)

- 2 short sleeve shirt
- 2 convertible shorts/pants
- 4 pairs lightweight wool socks
- swimsuit
- sun hat
- underwear
- laundry bags used to separate clothing in our panniers
- sewing repair kit

Cold Weather Gear (per person)

- fleece jacket
- long underwear top
- long underwear bottom
- mid-layer/wool long-sleeved top
- cold weather hat
- long fingered gloves

Rain Gear (per person)

- wind/rain jacket
- waterproof socks
- waterproof helmet covers

Shoes (per person)

- bike shoes
- walking shoes
- sandals

Documents and Money

- money belt
- credit card/s
- ATM debit card/s
- travelers checks
- small calculator
- local currency
- maps
- travel/guide books
- passports/visas/permits
- copies of important documents
- vaccination records
- driver's licenses
- small note pad and pen

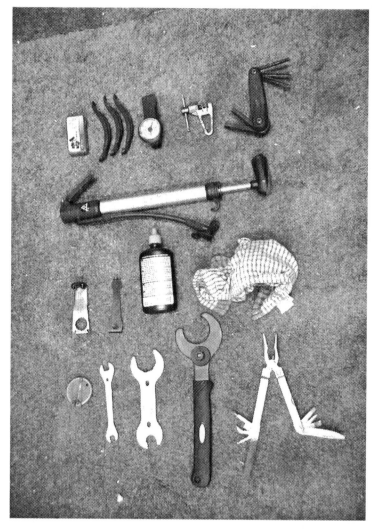

Bicycle tools.

Equipment List

Security

- combination pad lock for hostel lockers
- combination cable lock for bikes
- emergency stash of US currency

Tools (carried between us)

- patch kit
- tire levers
- tire pump
- tire pressure gauge
- chain tool
- allen key set
- cassette cracker (remover)
- chain ring bolt wrench
- cone wrench if not using sealed cartridge hubs
- chain lube/rag
- spoke wrench
- 8 and 10 mm wrench
- pedal - 32 mm headset wrench if not using thread-less system
- crank puller/bottom bracket tool
- multi tool/knife - (blade, pliers, screwdrivers, needle nose pliers, file, etc.)

Spare parts and repair kits

- one folding spare tire
- spare tubes, (number depends on the continent)
- shift/brake cable
- shift/brake cable housing
- spare brake pads
- spare spokes
- bike grease
- frame bolts
- short chain replacement section with extra joining links
- electrical. tape
- zip ties

Other

- laundry cord and detergent
- pillow
- mini binoculars
- recreational reading books
- English/Spanish dictionary
- small calculator

Peruvian girls walking home.

Tim ready to climb in Peru.